Framing referendum campaigns in the news

MANCHESTER
1824

Manchester University Press

Framing referendum campaigns in the news

MARINA DEKAVALLA

Manchester University Press

The right of Marina Dekavalla to be identified as the author of this work has been asserted by her in accordance with the Copyright, Designs and Patents Act 1988.

Published by Manchester University Press
Altrincham Street, Manchester M1 7JA
www.manchesteruniversitypress.co.uk

British Library Cataloguing-in-Publication Data
A catalogue record for this book is available from the British Library

ISBN 978 1 5261 1989 6 hardback
ISBN 978 1 5261 4367 9 paperback

First published by Manchester University Press in hardback 2018
This edition published 2019

The publisher has no responsibility for the persistence or accuracy of URLs for any external or third-party internet websites referred to in this book, and does not guarantee that any content on such websites is, or will remain, accurate or appropriate.

Typeset by Out of House Publishing

Contents

Figures and tables

Figures

Tables

Acknowledgements

I am grateful to the Economic and Social Research Council, which funded the research for this book through the Future Research Leaders scheme (grant number ES/L010062/1). Without their support this work would not have been possible.

I am also grateful to Professor Matthew Hibberd, for all his support during the project. I would also like to thank Professor Neil Blain for his very insightful feedback on early drafts of the manuscript for this book.

Many thanks also to Professor Claes de Vreese and his colleagues at the Amsterdam School of Communication Research, University of Amsterdam; Dr Enric Castelló, Dr Marta Montagut and their colleagues at Rovira i Virgili University, Tarragona; and Professor Michele Sorice and his colleagues at Luiss University, Rome, who gave me the opportunity to present early findings of this research during my visits to their institutions in 2015. Also many thanks to the anonymous reviewers of both the proposal for this book and the related journal articles that resulted from the same research.

I would like to thank all my interviewees from BBC Scotland and STV, the broadcasting regulator, the political communicators from both sides of the Scottish referendum debate, and the civil society representatives who kindly took the time to meet me and answer my questions. The 2014 Scottish referendum was a sensitive subject and I am truly grateful that so many key participants in the debate agreed to speak with me so shortly after the event, in early 2015. Many thanks also to those who were not interviewed themselves but helped me reach some of these interviewees, as well as the very patient administrators at BBC Scotland and STV who helped me arrange the interviews around everyone's very busy schedules. I would also like to thank BBC Scotland for providing me with copies of earlier campaign coverage in 2013, outside what I had in my own archive, which allowed me to draw comparisons with the analysis of the end of the campaign.

On a personal level, I would like to thank my mother, my partner and my friends for all their love, patience and support. They have made this book possible with their continuous encouragement.

Some of the findings and analysis reported in this book were previously published in different form in the following two journals. Tables 1 and 2 and Figure 1 appeared in the same form as in this book in article (b) below; Figure 2 and many of the quotes from interviews in chapters 3 and 5 appeared in the same form as in this book in article (a):

(a) Dekavalla, M. Issue and game frames in the news: Frame building factors in television coverage of the 2014 Scottish independence referendum. *Journalism*, published online ahead of print, pp. 1–20. Copyright © 2016 by the Author.

(b) Dekavalla, M. Framing referendum campaigns: The 2014 Scottish independence referendum in the press. *Media, Culture and Society*, 38(6): 793–810. Copyright © 2016 by the Author. Reprinted by permission of SAGE Publications, Ltd.

Introduction

Referendums are an increasingly used form of direct democracy internationally, even though within individual states they tend to be rare, one-off occasions. In just the last two years prior to the time of writing, referendums were organised to decide whether the UK would remain or leave the European Union (2016), the legalisation of same-sex marriage in Ireland (2015), the financing of political parties, the interpretation of taxation law and the structure of election constituencies in Poland (2015), lowering the age of voting and allowing foreign nationals to vote in Luxemburg (2015), accepting EU austerity proposals in Greece (2015), oil and natural gas drilling in Italy (2016), ratifying the peace agreement for the termination of the conflict between the government and the guerrilla military movement in Colombia (2016), and the Ukraine–European Union Association agreement in the Netherlands (2016), to name but a few of the diverse issues put to the public vote.

In many of these cases, referendum issues were too highly contested for political elites to legislate and consulting the electorate directly was seen as enabling a more straightforward resolution. The outcomes of most of these referendums have had important implications in their respective countries. For instance, the UK's 2016 EU referendum, instigated the most radical change in the country's relationship with the rest of Europe since the 1970s. Colombia's 2016 referendum, on the other hand, could have concluded a fifty-year long conflict, had the proposals not been rejected.

For these reasons referendums matter. It is particularly important to analyse the communication processes that frame referendums in the public domain, and more specifically in the mass media, which in modern democracies are the key platforms of political deliberation and opinion formation. This book analyses mediation practices during a recent referendum as an example, to help us understand the broader process by which the mass media define or frame what a contested political event is about.

This book aims to explain the media framing process in referendum campaigns as a distinctive category of political event. It looks at how the way journalists perform their daily work may impact on the way they construct political issues for their audiences. To address this aim, the book Introduces an original frame-building analytical model (in chapter 6) to account more broadly for how the media frame and reframe their sources' perspectives on what is at stake within the context of highly contested referendum campaigns. The discussion in chapter 6 explores how this model may help us interpret political mediation in referendums in Western and/or Northern European contexts. The model thus makes a contribution to wider debates around the coverage of referendum campaigns in the media.

Much of what the book discusses is not unique to referendums but applies to the mediation of politics more broadly and of election campaigns more specifically. Throughout the book the discussion draws from and contributes to these larger academic debates. However, for reasons that will be explained later in this chapter, referendums deserve separate attention as they are a special kind of event, one of the few instances of direct participatory politics in today's mass representative democracies. They are thus outside the regular experience of most citizens and for this reason how the media explain what they are about becomes even more significant.

The question at the heart of the concept of framing is what is at stake, or 'what is going on here?' Framing was introduced into social sciences from psychology, where it originally referred to 'individual frames', namely how we define an issue, situation or event in our minds by focusing on some of its aspects over others and using them as cues to understand what is happening. To use one of Goffman's (1974) examples, a woman looking carefully at a mirror may be understood by an observer to either be inspecting it in order to determine its condition before an auction, or to be looking at her own reflection. Which definition of the situation we choose in observing this scene will determine our understanding of why she is there, our expectations of what she will do next, what are the possible outcomes of the situation and even what might be an appropriate thing to say or do if we were to approach her. Which frame we choose will therefore determine 'a particular causal explanation' of the situation (why she is there), 'evaluation' of the possible outcomes, and 'treatment recommendation' – what, if anything, we should do or say (Entman, 1993: 52). Which frame we choose to apply will likely be determined by which aspects of what we see we choose to focus on. The concept of framing has been adapted in its application to the collective, social level in the study of politics and the media, as will be discussed in chapter 1, but its core essence as an organising principle that helps interpret events remains.

A key premise in framing is that social reality is constructed and reproduced through symbolic forms, such as language and images, which are the key components of media messages. Frame analysis is a relatively recent addition to an intellectual tradition of structuralist studies of the media, seeking in the analysis of text the key to the systems and processes of social signification and representation (Curran *et al.*, 1982: 19). If ideology, in an Althusserian understanding of the term, consists in the unconscious themes or categories through which people experience and represent the world and construct reality as social practice (Curran *et al.*, 1982), the study of frames is essentially a study of ideology.

However frame analysis does not share a view of frames as 'a motivated distortion of the truth', which is implicit in common sense understandings of ideology (Bennett, 1982: 44). In other words, there are not considered to be any 'true' interpretations of the world that are purposefully 'distorted' to perpetuate 'class domination', as in Marxist approaches to ideology. Rather different frames are seen as being promoted by different social groups and competing with each other for prominence in the public sphere and in the attention of journalists and audiences. Chapter 2 will discuss debates around journalistic frame-building in more detail as well as research on the effects of framing on audiences. It will also discuss how framing fits within normative debates on what the media should do to promote democratic citizenry.

The role of the media in offering the electorate information during a political campaign is very significant. In modern democracies the size of the electorate does not allow for face-to-face deliberation among all its members and deliberative democracy, understood as opinion formation and decision-making by citizens through public discussion and argumentation (Elster, 1998), is primarily realised through the media, which also feed frames into personal conversations and deliberations among citizens in the public sphere. For most people, the media are a key source of information on all political matters. They are even more important during major democratic events such as elections and referendums, while modern campaigns take place primarily through the media (Dalton, 2002) and are tailored to their needs.

The media landscape in much of the Western world has changed significantly in the last decades with the growth and wide adoption of digital media. However, traditional news outlets such as television and the press have retained a significant part in the 'relay race' of discourses in the public sphere (Garton *et al.*, 1991: 100–103), whereby print, broadcast and online media co-create public debate and re-represent discourse on different platforms. For this reason traditional media, like television and newspapers, remain significant in the digital era. Although, since the establishment of the print press, other media have been added and even took over prominence as significant loci for political discourse in the public sphere, none of these platforms operates in isolation. Different media platforms feed from and into each other and together they construct and reconstruct public sense making.

This book thus focuses on 'traditional' or 'old' media, and seeks to address research questions on how frames emerge on these media during referendum campaigns, how these frames differ from the frames that define electoral contests, what factors may influence journalistic selection and adoption among the frames that are available in the public sphere and promoted by different interest groups, and whether journalists have an active role in creating original frames themselves when covering referendums. The empirical component of the study is based on the case of the 2014 Scottish independence referendum, but previous analyses of different referendums in other countries are brought into focus to compare findings and derive broader insights into the process of framing referendums as distinctive political events.

These insights form the basis of the frame-building model for referendums, which is proposed in chapter 6. The book thus goes beyond the specific case study and proposes a new way of understanding frame-building in referendum campaigns, which can be applied and tested in other national contexts.

Although referendums are often seen as similar to election campaigns, they are significantly distinctive events and deserve separate analysis. Their purpose is not to elect a government but to consult the electorate on a divisive issue; the result of the vote does not directly affect who is to be in power; referendums are one-offs, not regular events; there may not be clear correspondence between party identification and ideological stance, as there often is in elections; parties may cluster in unexpected coalitions, supporting the same side of a referendum question whereas otherwise their political agendas may clash (de Vreese and Semetko, 2004).

Referendums remain one of the few commonly used forms of direct democracy. Mechanisms of direct democracy may be defined as 'a publicly recognized institution wherein citizens decide or emit their opinion on issues – other than through legislative and executive elections – directly at the ballot box through universal and secret suffrage' (Altman, 2011: 7). Direct democracy mechanisms include referendums, but also plebiscites, citizen initiatives and recalls of elected officials. Direct democracy allows citizens to decide on divisive issues directly rather than through their representatives. Representative democracy, on the other hand, is based on citizens electing representatives at regular intervals to make decisions on behalf of their constituents, or according to another view, on behalf of the 'common', national good (Cronin, 1989: 26). Representative democracy systems often make use of direct democracy mechanisms in exceptional circumstances, so the two ways of decision-making are complementary rather than conflicting.

Still, the usefulness of direct democracy mechanisms has been disputed. Those who argue against the use of referendums as an instrument of decision-making claim that referendums can allow elite groups to manipulate public opinion and use direct democracy for their own benefit, that they weaken the role of elected officials, that they privilege the rule of minorities by the majority, that ordinary people do not have the 'competence' to make important political decisions and they sometimes vote against their own interests. On the other hand, proponents of referendums stress their capacity to increase citizens' interest in public affairs and their control in decision-making, to enhance accountability, to train people in self-government and civil awareness, to resolve difficult issues fairly and transparently (Cronin, 1989; Butler and Ramney, 1994; Altman, 2011; Tierney, 2012).

Proponents of direct democracy mechanisms argue that a combination of the two forms of democracy, with referendums being called occasionally to allow citizens to decide on specific issues, actually helps representative democracy work better. According to Altman (2011: 197), in mature democracies referendums work as 'a legitimization tool for constitutional changes that occasionally serve as a synchronization mechanism between politicians and citizens' and do not compromise the quality of democratic rule. Qvortrup (2014: 12) associates the increasingly common adoption of referendums to a de-alignment in recent history between political parties and the needs of civic and minority groups, as well as a growing feeling among the electorate that parties are not able to represent them. He suggests that the role of referendums is often to relieve the political system from individual groups' demands, which may not be supported by the majority of citizens but which may still put pressure on governments. As he puts it, in those cases referendums act as a pressure valve, letting off political steam, while at the same time they help rebuild trust in the democratic system and remove controversial issues from the political agenda. The role of governments and elite political groups in shaping discourse during referendums will be examined in detail in subsequent chapters.

This book analyses coverage of the 2014 Scottish independence referendum in television and newspapers, as well as insights from interviews with television reporters, heads of television news departments and public affairs producers, broadcasting regulators, political campaign managers, and civic society representatives who remained neutral in the referendum but communicated with the media during the campaign to promote issues that were significant to their specific groups.

The aim of the analysis is to explain how the media select, reproduce or reconstruct ways of understanding what referendum campaigns are about, based on the direct experience of actors who participated in this process. It contributes to our understanding of which frames become prominent in political coverage by detailing how specific factors relating to journalists, their professional values, their organisations and their relationships with their political sources may combine with each other to promote particular interpretations of what is at stake.

Each referendum has unique features determined by the national context, political culture and media system as well as the particularities of the issue itself, how much it has been previously debated in the public arena, how political elites cluster around the possible options and how fixed public opinion is on this issue (LeDuc, 2002: 145). Acknowledging that different contexts give rise to different dynamics in the media coverage of a referendum, chapter 6 attempts to identify broad similarities between the media framing of the Scottish referendum and that of other, rather diverse campaigns. It discusses these similarities within the context of common characteristics shared by the media systems where similar studies have taken place, and proposes an original framework, which expands understanding of journalistic frame-building in highly contested referendums within these media systems.

The 2014 Scottish referendum was a historic occasion. As voters went to polling stations on 18 September 2014 there was a clear sense that they were participating in a rare event that was likely to have a lasting impact on the structure of the United Kingdom irrespective of the outcome. Participation in the vote was unprecedented – 84.6 per cent of registered voters turned out, an exception to the well-established trend of political apathy that came to typify political life in the UK, as in many other Western states in previous decades. In the two years of campaigning that led to September 2014, the referendum succeeded in capturing the hearts and minds of Scots like few other political events, it dominated conversations not only in the media, but also in homes, workplaces and pubs, equally among supporters of independence and the union as among those who were still undecided.

Eventually 55 per cent of the electorate decided that Scotland should stay in the UK. Although after the referendum, the debate on Scottish independence continued and it is still a current topic on the political agenda at the time of writing (in the aftermath of the 2016 EU referendum and the Brexit negotiations there is talk of a second Scottish independence referendum), when the 2014 referendum took place it was widely described by politicians on both sides as a once-in-a-lifetime opportunity to have a say on this issue. There was a widespread sense that even if one had little other interest in politics, the Scottish referendum was too critical an issue on which not to have an informed opinion. Like the 2016 EU referendum two years later, the Scottish referendum was a major event in the constitutional history of the UK. As I will argue in the final chapter of this book, the way that the media approached these two events is not dissimilar.

The question on the ballot paper in 2014 was simple and binary: should Scotland be an independent country? It included no suggestion or implication of what criteria should be applied to choose between answering yes or no. As with most referendum questions its phrasing was negotiated between the key political players, in this case the UK and Scottish governments, and was shaped so as to allow different definitions of what exactly was at stake and what independence would mean in practice. These definitions were to be provided by political actors with a stake in the debate, by the mass media, and by citizens themselves.

During the referendum grassroots groups reinvigorated the debate on social media and challenged the dominance of 'old' news platforms (Law, 2015; Buchanan, 2016), but at the same time the press and broadcasting remained central 'in setting the parameters of official political discourse as well as registering the ways in which social media replicate the established patterns of political discourse as much as it threatens to dislodge them' (Law, 2015: 7). The issues dominating the debate on 'old' media were also the main material for discussion on social media (Paterson, 2015: 23).

In 2014, 92 per cent of UK adults reported watching television almost every day (Ofcom, 2015) and television was the most used source for news (Reuters Institute for the Study of Journalism, 2015). Newspapers may have had a restricted print readership (the Scottish press had been losing readers at a faster rate than newspapers in other parts of the UK during the previous decade – see Dekavalla, 2015), but they were still read by political elites and by contributors to broadcast and online media, and they often became themselves direct or indirect contributors to conversations on other platforms. Although digital media were very important in the campaign, at the time studied here 'traditional media organisations continue[d] to play a pivotal role in British politics' (Chadwick and Stanyer, 2011: 216) as primary and credible sources of political information, co-creators of public discourse and the main way for social actors to reach a large audience. The continuing relevance of 'old' media in the digital era returned into focus in the 2016 EU referendum, where newspapers are said to have reinforced anti-European sentiment in public debate.

UK media operate according to a liberal media system (Hallin and Mancini, 2004). The press is commercial and highly partisan, while both public service and commercial broadcasting has a public service role and is bound by rules of due impartiality. Newspapers take explicit positions in favour or against political actors and causes, as will be seen in detail in chapter 2. In the case of the 2014 referendum, all newspapers adopted a sceptical position towards Scottish independence during the campaign, apart from the *Sunday Herald*, which was the only title that came out in favour of the Yes campaign a few weeks before the vote. Broadcasting, on the other hand, operates under the regulatory obligation to provide a fair opportunity for a range of perspectives to be heard, and cannot take a position in any debate. As will be explained in subsequent chapters, however, the issue of television's impartiality became a contested one during the campaign. The final section of chapter 2 provides a detailed discussion of the media outlets analysed in this study and their individual characteristics in terms of ownership and positioning.

The next chapter, however, takes a step away from the Scottish case to discuss framing as a broader theory of understanding media content and political communication in general. It reviews key themes in frame analysis and discusses previous work on the framing of political campaigns in different contexts. It also explores existing research on the generic frames commonly found in the coverage of political campaigns, and particularly of elections. Research exploring the conditions that give rise to such generic frames is also reviewed, with a view to establishing what may be learned from this research for the analysis of referendum campaigns.

Chapter 3 returns to the Scottish case and provides a contextual overview of the historic events that led to the 2014 referendum. It offers a summary of how the Scottish constitutional issue developed particularly in the second half of the twentieth century, the movement for devolution in the 1990s, the establishment and the first decade of the devolved Scottish parliament, up until the 2011 Scottish election, which instigated the independence referendum. It also discusses definitions of Scottish identity and their role in claims for Scottish independence. It then maps out the media landscape in Scotland and the media's ideological positions in relation to autonomy.

Chapter 4 focuses on the key actors who ran communication campaigns during the referendum, aiming to attract media attention to their views. It focuses particularly on the main Yes and No campaigns and the political parties that comprised them, as well as civil society organisations that did not support either outcome but still communicated to the media about issues they felt were significant in the debate. The chapter discusses the frames these participant actors promoted in the public debate. It is based on interviews with communication directors on both sides of the argument and representatives from impartial civil society organisations. It explores how different actors understood and defined what the referendum was about and how these understandings may be organised conceptually into different frames. It looks at similarities, differences and interactions between the frames that different actors proposed and explores whether different sides of the argument had 'ownership' over certain frames.

Chapter 5 looks at which frames were most prominent in the media coverage of the referendum. The frames identified earlier are traced in the coverage of the end of the campaign on BBC Scotland and STV, the two broadcasters that produce dedicated content for audiences in Scotland. This is complemented by an analysis of newspaper articles in ten Scottish daily and Sunday newspapers. The *strategic game* and *policy* frames were the two most dominant frames in both television and newspaper coverage, with the *game* frame becoming more prominent as the referendum date approached. The chapter concludes by discussing the democratic implications of representing the referendum as a strategic competition between political sides and as a decision about policy.

The subsequent chapter attempts to explain the prominence of these frames in the media coverage, based on insights from interviews with broadcasters and their sources. It proposes five factors which played a role in shaping media frames: the influence of political campaigns, professional routines relating to balance, journalists' views of their own role in the coverage of a contested issue, broadcasters' perceptions of what attracts audiences and what constitutes a contribution to public debate, as well as previous experience of covering election campaigns. The discussion is contextualised within broader academic literature about frame-building.

After these four chapters, which explore the particular case study, chapter 6 and the conclusion shift their attention to how the insights generated from this analysis may help understand the broader issue of the mediation of politics, beyond the Scottish context.

Chapter 6 compares insights from the previous chapters with those from other framing studies in different contexts and discusses the extent to which certain frames may be expected to emerge in the coverage of referendum campaigns in general, as a broader category of political event. Comparisons are drawn to research focusing on the 1980 Quebec independence referendum, the 2000 euro referendum in Denmark and the 2008 Swiss direct-democratic consultation on immigration, which are the other case studies where media framing studies have been carried out. The chapter identifies connections between the similarities these cases share and the characteristics of the media systems where they are located. These similarities form the basis of an frame-building model for referendum campaigns, which is proposed in this chapter to help explain how the media cover referendums in these media systems.

Finally, the concluding chapter revisits the question of whether the mediation of referendum campaigns is distinctive enough to deserve dedicated analysis. It queries the extent to which the referendum analysed in this book bears similarities with the UK's subsequent 2016 EU referendum and how that event was framed in the mainstream media. The chapter argues that the frame-building model proposed in chapter 6 appears to also provide an account for the mediation of that campaign. The chapter concludes with a wider consideration of the contribution of old and new media to our understanding of politics. It considers the changing nature of public debate following Brexit and the 2016 US presidential election and questions the extent to which mainstream media remain key determinants of public discourse. It proposes that future avenues for frame-building research would need to explore frame-building processes on social media, where the gatekeepers and organisational routines that are so central in the frame-building model proposed in chapter 6 are absent. It argues that in order to deliver the complete picture frame analysis needs to engage with the totality of news provision and sharing as this moves towards the internet and news aggregation, propaganda sites and social media.

I

Framing political campaigns

Frames and frame-building in the media

> The procedure is actually quite simple. First you arrange things into different groups. Of course, one pile may be sufficient depending upon how much there is to do. If you have to go somewhere else due to lack of facilities that is the next step, otherwise you are pretty well set. It is important not to overdo things. That is, it is better to do too few things at once than too many. In the short run this may not seem important but complications can easily arise. A mistake can be expensive as well. At first the whole procedure will seem complicated. Soon, however, it will simply become just another facet of life. It is difficult to foresee any end to the necessity for this task in the immediate future, but one can never tell. After the procedure is completed one arranges the materials into different groups again. Then they can be put into the appropriate places. Eventually they will be used once more and the whole cycle will have to be repeated. However, that is a part of life. (Cappella and Jamieson, 1997: 42)

The above excerpt was used in cognitive psychology experiments by Bransford and Johnson (1972: 722) who showed that understanding and remembering a complex piece of text becomes easier when the topic of the narrative is introduced before reading it. This excerpt was difficult for experiment participants to understand without any cues, but when it was introduced with the explanation that the topic discussed was doing the laundry, comprehension significantly improved. This was because subjects brought in their previous knowledge of what using a washing machine involves to influence their interpretation of the specific situation described here. The script of what usually happens when one does the laundry and the personal experience of doing it oneself not only provide referents for abstract words in the text, like 'things' and 'facilities', but also help understand why 'at first the procedure will seem complicated'. The concept of doing the laundry frames our understanding of the text: it provides us with an idea to help us organise our making sense of what is going on (Gamson and Modigliani, 1989).

Cappella and Jamieson borrow this example to explain how applying a frame on an event activates the reader's pre-existing knowledge and experience, which work together with what is there in the text to create an interpretation of the event described. This interpretation also invokes inferences regarding the causes and expectations about the possible outcomes of the event, which do not need to be stated in the text because they are provided by the reader. In this way frames 'serve as an explicit context within which texts are interpreted' (Cappella and Jamieson, 1997: 42).

The above discussion helps understand what is probably the most used definition of framing in the social sciences. To frame is 'to select some aspects of a perceived reality and make them more salient in a communicating text, in such a way as to promote a particular problem definition, causal interpretation, moral evaluation, and/or treatment recommendation' (Entman, 1993: 52). Frames are schemata, which define, or put a label on, an event or issue by focusing on certain of its aspects. For instance, a conflict frame will focus on the aspects of an event that make it similar to a conflict. This event may at the same time also have aspects that make it similar to a consultation, but the conflict frame will detract attention from these by labeling the event as a conflict.

By defining an event as a conflict (problem definition), the frame in turn evokes our previous knowledge of what happens during a conflict and what causes a conflict (causal interpretation). It invites us to apply moral evaluations to the event that we would normally apply to a conflict and connects the possible outcomes of this event with the possible outcomes of a conflict – therefore the possible solutions (or treatment recommendations) are the ones we would expect in a conflict. By applying to the event considerations we would normally associate with a conflict, the frame invites us to think about the event in this way – just as the laundry frame invites us to think about the situation described at the start of the chapter by combining what is there in the text with our own previous experiences and expectations of doing the laundry. In both cases, the frame provides 'a central organizing idea or story line that provides meaning to an unfolding strip of events, weaving a connection among them' (Gamson and Modigliani, 1987: 143).

As discussed in the first chapter, although the choice or promotion of one frame over another may be based on ideological grounds and can have ideological implications, a frame is essentially an organisational principle for an issue or event, not a value system. In other words ideology as a value system may guide our selection of frames, but frames themselves are ways of organising, communicating and grasping the meaning of specific situations.

As Price *et al.* (1997) suggest, frames make connections of 'applicability', namely they apply considerations, which are relevant to one problem, to questions about another, for example considerations which are relevant to doing the laundry are applied to the situation the reader of the earlier excerpt is dealing with; or, according to Nisbet (2010), they 'suggest a connection between two concepts, issues, or things, such that after exposure to the framed message, audiences accept or are at least aware of the connection'.

Frames are essential both in making sense of a situation and telling a story about it to others – thus they are an essential part of how media narratives negotiate meaning with audiences. In most events and issues several frames, promoted by different social actors, compete to become prominent in media discourse. As Hall suggests, the definition 'of events is part of what has to be struggled over, for it is the means by which collective social understandings are created' (1982: 65). Clearly, as will be discussed in the section on framing effects below, high prominence of a frame in media discourse does not automatically entail its adoption by audiences, because audiences' own values and knowledge are also important in their making sense of public issues. Still the media hold a very significant role in proposing frames for audiences to consider.

Theorists (Entman, 1993; Scheufele, 1999) distinguish between 'individual' frames (cognitive schemata of interpretation at the individual level) and 'media' frames (organising schemata that turn occurrences into meaningful events within media reports) – yet these are linked and impact on each other. In the model proposed by Scheufele (1999) the media build frames influenced by factors internal and external to news organisations, but in doing this they draw from among socially available interpretations of an issue. Media framing influences the perceived importance of certain frames over others among the public, which in turn influences people's interpretations and attitudes at the individual level and feed into public debates and public opinion. As journalists are themselves also members of the public, their interpretations are also influenced at the individual level by media frames. These individual interpretations combine with the other organisational, professional and extra-media or societal influences journalists receive in their professional capacity and thus the circle of framing continues.

The circular process of framing – which involves the media, their sources, the public as well as social institutions and societal ideologies external to the media – determines the goals of the social scientist in studying framing. These are to identify different frames and the framing devices that carry them and demonstrate their presence in media texts;

to explain how these frames came to be included in media narratives; to explore how media frames interact with people's previous knowledge to shape understandings of issues and events in the news; and to determine how these understandings influence public opinion (D'Angelo, 2002).

Much research on framing has focused on the effects of the media, namely the third (and by extension also the fourth) stage of the process described above. Price *et al.* (1997: 486) define a framing effect as 'one in which salient attributes of a message (its organization, selection of content, or thematic structure) render particular thoughts applicable, resulting in their activation and use in evaluations'. Research on how such effects take place in experimental and real-life conditions is extensive and will be discussed in a dedicated section later in this chapter. Indeed, framing is seen by many as primarily a theory that accounts for media effects (Cacciatore *et al.*, 2016).

However, the stage of the framing process whereby frames are created, selected and included in media narratives – what Scheufele (1999) has named frame building – has traditionally received less attention by comparison (Tandoc, 2015). In his own theoretical account, Scheufele proposes that 'at least five factors may potentially influence how journalists frame a given issue: social norms and values, organizational pressures and constraints, pressures of interest groups, journalistic routines, and ideological or political orientations of journalists' (1999: 109). Yet the ways in which such factors may interact in real empirical situations have remained relatively unexplored, at least compared to the breadth of research that has focused on framing effects.

A theoretical piece of work that provided a more systematic classification of what may consist such factors is Shoemaker and Reese's (2014) model of influences on journalistic content. Although their account is not specifically intended as a contribution to framing theory per se, and is about the creation of journalistic content more broadly, it provides a comprehensive critical overview and integration of previous journalism sociology research, which explores factors that influence how media content is produced and shaped. Based on this discussion, Shoemaker and Reese (2014) propose a classification of these factors along five different levels: at the individual level (journalists' personal beliefs and values), the routines level (the standardised professional practices of journalism), the organisational level (the impact of media companies, their structures and ownership), the social institution level (the relationships between the media and other powerful institutions), and the social systems level (ideological and cultural influences from the social system as a whole).

Their model is a useful analytical tool that acknowledges that different influences interact with each other in shaping the output of the media – so several influences at different levels are always at play. It offers a conceptual mapping, which empirical studies may adapt to discuss different aspects of news making in a range of contexts. It thus lends itself particularly well for structuring studies of frame building, and how particular frames come to predominate in the coverage of specific issues and events in traditional media. Critics have suggested that it does not account for the diminished role of traditional professional routines in online media (Keith, 2011) and one of the authors themselves proposed that the model is not meant to 'capture all of the complex interrelationships involved in the media' (Reese, 2007: 31). Still, Shoemaker and Reese's model remains a very useful tool to help organise our thinking around the frame-building process.

Brüggemann (2014), for example, uses this model to theorise factors on different levels that may impact on whether journalists will create their own original interpretations of an issue or event they are reporting on (frame setting) or reproduce the frames of their sources without interfering (frame sending). He believes that instead of being two polar opposites, these two options form the ends of a continuum and most journalists will do both to different degrees, depending on factors on different levels of Shoemaker and Reese's model. Therefore, for instance, if a journalist has strong opinions and personal values on a specific issue at the individual level, he/she may be more likely to set his/her own frames, and this tendency will be even stronger if, at the organisational level, his/her opinions are supported by newsroom colleagues. Brüggemann proposes that how exactly factors at different levels combine should be explored in empirical studies of specific contexts, to provide a richer account of frame-building. Chapter 6 of this book explores this question in the context of the Scottish referendum.

Castelló and Montagut (2011) propose, in a similar vein, that journalists to some extent always 'reframe' issues and events before they present them to their audiences, namely they contextualise, transform and reconfigure the frames promoted by their sources, but the degree to which they do this varies between 'weak' and 'strong' reframers. In their interviews, radio journalists in Catalonia suggested that they use material given to them by politicians but adapt it based on news values such as controversy and entertainment, and on professional norms such as the need for ideological balance. Similar findings were established in interviews with journalists in other countries as well: news values, editorial lines, professional ideals, access to and relationship with sources, peer influence, the familiarity of frames from previous debates, and exclusive access to stories, all seem to have an influence on frame-building in different national contexts and types of news events (Bartholomé *et al.*, 2015; Boesman *et al.*, 2015; Kothari, 2010; Tandoc, 2015).

A different vein of research has sought to account for frame-building through content analysis of journalistic output and/or of publicity material provided by news sources (for instance Bedingfield and Anshari, 2014; Hanggli, 2012), rather than through interviews with journalists. These studies provide significant evidence that the frames of powerful sources do permeate media coverage, yet they do not seek to explain how this occurs according to the direct experience of news content producers. As Brüggemann (2014) argues, in order to connect the frames found in the news to the context they were created in, we need to analyse both media content and journalists' own experience as frame-builders.

In its analysis of the framing of the 2014 Scottish referendum in subsequent chapters, this book explores the connection between the context of production and news content. It does this by explaining frame-building during a highly contested referendum campaign through the perspectives of the actors who were involved in the coverage as well as by analysing the coverage itself. Later in this chapter I will discuss what insights from previous research tell us about how the media frame different types of political campaigns, but first the next two sections will explore why the way that the media frame referendums matters in the first place.

The media and political decision-making: normative approaches

Frames are particularly relevant in the coverage of political issues, where multiple interpretations are possible of what is going on and what is at stake. Frames matter in politics because, as Kinder puts it, they 'suggest how politics should be thought about', 'what the essential issue is' and, therefore, 'what, if anything, should be done' (2007: 156).

In modern mass democracies, where face-to-face deliberation is not possible due to the size of the electorate, the mass media have become the locus of deliberative democracy, namely the locus of opinion formation and decision-making through public discussion and argumentation (Elster, 1998). The media are therefore the key platform where frames compete for prominence in political life and thus they carry particular significance during democratic decision-making events, such as elections and referendums.

Before moving to examine how the media may frame these decision-making political events, it is important to explore how expectations regarding the role of the media in deliberative democracy have shaped this kind of empirical enquiry. Normative accounts of the role of the media in deliberative democracy ascribe obligations that journalism should fulfil – according to theorists – in order to facilitate citizens in fulfilling their role in a well-functioning democracy. Such normative assumptions often underlie studies that seek to assess or to better understand media performance in the coverage of specific elections or referendums. At the same time, normative perceptions about what democracy is and how the media may facilitate its function also shape journalists' own views of their role and what constitutes 'good' journalism (Skovsgaard et al., 2013).

There are two main schools of thought regarding the normative role of the media in deliberative democracy, each based on a different view of the role of citizenship in political life and the extent to which citizens are expected to take active part in it: the liberal and the popular inclusion approaches. In the subsequent paragraphs I will explain the key positions of each one and I will then argue that the liberal approach places political elites as the key frame-builders of media messages, while the popular inclusion approach requires journalists to take on a more active role in setting new frames and in questioning the frames promoted by elites.

In the liberal approach citizens have a relatively restricted role in democracy. They express their opinion every few years by electing their representatives and thus legitimising government rule. The elected policy-makers are ultimately accountable to the electorate, but otherwise citizens do not not have much direct involvement in regular public debate on public issues (Curran, 1991; Crespi, 1997; Hackett, 2005). This approach is based on the assumption that ordinary people do not have the time, ability or the interest to understand complex political issues and their role should be limited to electing the specialists-politicians who will then shape public policy (Lippmann, 1922). In liberal theory public debate should be dominated by the representatives of the electorate and experts who offer their 'impartial' and 'scientific' perspectives. The views of these actors compete for prominence and for public support in a 'marketplace' of ideas.

According to Hackett (2005), there are two forms of this liberalist model: market liberalism, which sees the laws of the free market as determining all aspects of political communication, and public sphere liberalism, which prioritises the expression of a wide range of different interests in the public sphere. Public sphere liberalism is influenced by Habermas's (1989) conceptualisation of a communicative space, a forum within society where citizens form their opinions about issues of common concern, by participating in a process of public deliberation and rational argumentation. Public opinion, which is understood as consensus arrived at through deliberation, legitimises government decisions and, in

Habermas's much debated and contested ideal, is formed through debate among 'equal' participants interested in the 'common good'. Essentially public sphere liberalism refers to a space for debate to which all (elites and non-elites; politicians and citizens) should have access but where the strongest and most convincing argument wins. Despite Habermas's original scepticism about the ability of the mass media to be this forum, in modern mass democracies they are by default the main locus where citizens can be exposed to political debate before forming their opinion. Although some (Hackett, 2005) see this discursive democratic model as one form of liberalism, others (Feree *et al.*, 2002) make a clear distinction between representative liberal theories, which exclude citizens from public debate, and Habermas's 'discursive' approach, which encourages citizen participation as a means to increase the amount of deliberation in the public sphere.

In liberal theory, the normative role the media should perform is to provide objective information that will help citizens make informed choices during election time and to encourage people to vote (Curran, 1991, 2000; Feree *et al.*, 2002). Such an understanding of the role of the media is reflected, for instance, in empirical research assessing whether and how the media contribute to 'informed citizenry'. An informed citizen is understood in this perspective as one who knows enough about what different groups of political elites propose to make a reasoned decision on who to vote for (Strömbäck, 2005). As will be seen in subsequent chapters, this is a rather dominant view within the media industry about the role of journalism in politics, especially among British broadcasters. In liberal democratic media systems, it has shaped professionals' notions of what it means to report fairly on an election or referendum. If the role of the media is to give citizens enough information to decide on how to vote, fairness means to provide equal space to different political groups to express their positions and to try and persuade voters, without interfering with the content of what is being said, and let audiences decide for themselves. Such a liberal view of the media has influenced notions of journalistic 'objectivity' and 'impartiality' in broadcasting, as will be discussed in chapter 5.

Critics of representative liberal views propose an alternative, participatory democratic approach. The participatory approach is more inclusive, supporting maximum participation of ordinary citizens, as well as marginalised social groups, in democracy (Crespi, 1997). In more radical versions of this approach, the public sphere is seen as an arena of power struggle between social groups with contrasting interests, who try to have their views heard and their discourses accepted in public debate (Curran, 2000; Hackett, 2005).

Feree *et al.* (2002) distinguish between two approaches that are based on popular inclusion: participatory liberal and constructionist theories both require citizen participation in politics. They both propose that the agenda of the debate should be continuously formed by the public. Their difference is that constructionist approaches particularly privilege the accounts of marginalised groups and encourage the integration of personal narratives in policy debate.

In general, theories which require citizen participation in the public sphere argue that the role of the media should be to provide access to public debate to a diversity of actors, non-elite as well as elite, and to promote active citizen involvement in politics. They believe that the more citizens participate in public debate the more competent they become in public matters (Feree *et al.*, 2002). Encouraging active forms of citizenry involves reporting diverse viewpoints and encouraging dialogue between them (Bennett *et al.*, 2004), raising awareness of injustices, presenting ordinary citizens as potential agents in solving their own problems and giving prominence to actors from civil society (Gamson, 2001), presenting citizens as contributing actively and substantially to debate and giving more coverage to polls and protests (Lewis *et al.*, 2005). As Schudson (1995) notes, a 'catalogue of available information' is not adequate for informed citizenry. An informed citizen, in this approach, is an engaged citizen who has an active role in political debate.

In essence, representative liberal theories and participatory approaches differ in where they locate power in democratic debate: the former believe in a public sphere where deliberation is dominated by the representatives of the people, namely politicians and other elites, while the latter see the involvement of ordinary citizens and of marginalised voices as crucial in democracy.

Which of these contrasting understandings of democracy one adopts has implications for normative expectations not only on the role of journalists in the public sphere (Strömbäck, 2005) but also on whose frames should emerge in the media. Simon and Xenos (2000) argue that media frames are very important in the public sphere because they are the principal means by which public debate takes place. In their view, competing frames emerge as different actors propose alternative ways of understanding an issue, and when frames decline in prominence this is an indication that competing claims have been explored in the discursive arena and resolved through public deliberation.

According to the liberal approach examined earlier, therefore, the frames that the media are expected to expose to the consideration of the public are those of the elites – politicians, major political campaigns and experts (Strömbäck, 2005). It is the role of elites – and not of the media – to determine what an issue or a political event is about and what aspects are relevant in thinking about it. In this approach, the media should reproduce elite framing and help voters choose between political opponents. The role of the public is to make a competent choice between policies proposed by the elites, which means to evaluate different competing elite frames as presented in the media and not be swayed by individual elite groups' attempts to manipulate public opinion (Druckman, 2001). By contrast, in a participatory democratic approach framing is bottom-up rather than top-down, the media are expected to represent the frames of the governed to the governing and to be more active in setting new, original frames contesting those sponsored by elites.

In a participatory democratic approach it may thus be expected that the media should be 'frame-setters', rather than 'frame-senders' (Brüggemann, 2014). This means that they would be expected to introduce new ways of understanding events and issues rather than reproduce those they receive from elite sources. This chapter will later look at previous research into the frames that tend to dominate media discourse in elections and referendums and discuss the extent to which this may be a realistic expectation. Before doing this though, and having so far considered normative, theory-based reasons why media framing matters, I will turn to address a central implication in most discussion of why media frames matter: the assumption that frames have an impact on what the public thinks.

The media and political decision-making: framing effects

Perhaps one of the greatest appeals of framing as an approach to analysing media content is its potential to connect media content with its effect on audiences. Even if not all framing studies explore frame effects (and indeed neither does this book), there tends to be a broader underlying assumption in much scholarship around frames that framing matters because it has an impact on how audiences understand events and issues and, perhaps, how they act in response to them.

Scheufele (1999) distinguishes between framing research where frames are dependent variables, namely studies that look at how frames emerge in discourse and why some become more prominent than others, and research where frames are independent variables. The latter include studies that explore whether and how media frames impact on how individuals understand issues, talk about them, evaluate issues and political actors and make political decisions. He distinguishes between two aspects of framing effects: frame salience (the ability of audiences to recall frames they encountered in the media) and frame importance (whether or not audiences accept these frames as valid or significant in their attitudes and decision-making).

Much framing effects research suggests that frames are influential: by emphasising specific aspects and rendering them more relevant than other aspects relating to an issue or event, frames direct audiences on how to think, interpret and talk about issues (Shah *et al.*, 1996; Tewksbury *et al.*, 2000; de Vreese, 2004). However, this process is not straightforward and the media are not all-powerful in determining audience frames.

The effects of framing emerge from an interaction between what individuals already know and believe about an issue and the frames presented in media messages (Baden and Lecheler, 2012). Druckman (2001) suggests that five factors moderate the power of framing effects: people's pre-existing positions, opinions and values; their political knowledge; deliberation with others in their immediate environment; the perceived credibility of frame sources; and the fact that people are naturally exposed to several competing frames rather than just one. For these reasons, he suggests, 'framing effects are remarkably complex. Sometimes they work and other times they do not' (Druckman, 2001: 246). This may explain why in referendum contexts media frames have been found to be salient in how people discuss events but this does not necessarily entail impact on their attitudes and voting intentions (Wettstein, 2012); in other words frame salience does not necessarily entail frame importance.

A number of studies have sought to resolve this complexity by clarifying the conditions in which framing is effective in shaping attitudes and those in which it is not. Bechtel *et al.* (2015), for example, show that voters in a Swiss referendum who were exposed to partisan framing at the end of a campaign did not change their opinions, but the media frames only reinforced their pre-existing convictions and voting intentions. This was even more the case among more politically knowledgeable voters. In fact, very knowledgeable and ignorant audiences are not easily affected by media framing and only those with some political knowledge may potentially be influenced (Slothuus, 2008; Lecheler and de Vreese, 2011). This is also confirmed by another study, which found that in a US proposition campaign where voters had less pre-existing knowledge about the issue, framing effects appeared to be stronger (Binder *et al.*, 2015). In addition to audiences' previous political knowledge, the personal values that an individual holds also play a role in whether or not his/her attitudes and voting behaviour will change after exposure to media frames (Schemer *et al.*, 2012).

Moreover, generic frames, such as the conflict and economic consequences frames, which do not carry inherent valence, have been shown

to impact the way audiences – and especially more politically knowledgeable audiences – speak about issues, but without influencing their
policy preferences and decisions (de Vreese, 2004). Even this influence
on how people understand and talk about issues can be temporary
and may wear out if audiences are not repeatedly exposed to the same
frames. For a framing effect to be durable, it needs to initiate changes
in a person's knowledge, provide new information and connections that
the person is not already familiar with, and these need to be retrieved
again at a later point in time – in other words the person needs to be able
to memorise these new connections and recall them (Baden and Lecheler,
2012). Apart from individual-level factors, though, contextual factors
(such as exposure to competing frames and interpersonal discussions
with others) are also influential in whether individuals adopt a frame or
not (Druckman, 2004).

The volume of sometimes conflicting research on framing effects does
not mean that framing effects do not exist. As Druckman (2004) suggests, framing effects do occur and must be taken seriously. However,
like in all attempts to explain media effects, there are many factors to
consider when exploring the process through which people form perceptions of the world, views and decisions. People are exposed to a range
of information sources and experiences over time, and new information,
whether it comes from the media or not, is processed within the context
of previously acquired information, knowledge, beliefs and attitudes,
as well as of information that is received simultaneously from different
sources.

Moreover, frames promoted by the media are not only influential directly at the individual level, on the specific members of the audience who
consume these media at a specific time, but additionally they feed into
and shape public discourse in the longer run. Public discourse around any
event or issue is produced collaboratively by a range of actors. Garton
et al. (1991: 100–103) propose that the public sphere (of a general election) is like a 'relay race' where discourses circulate between politicians
and the mass media like batons and statements are 're-presented in different discursive domains'. Although these authors do not discuss framing specifically, their conceptualisation of public debate usefully reminds
us that no source of information operates in a vacuum; and that framing is not necessarily uni-directional, from elites to the media to audiences, but multi-directional. A frame originating in one part of the public
sphere may influence how other parts of the public sphere talk about an
issue and thus may reach audiences indirectly.

For instance, during the Scottish referendum studied here, the frame
suggesting that the referendum was a decision about public policy was

widely promoted by both campaigns and the media (as will be seen in subsequent chapters) and this shaped opinion poll questions, run by independent pollsters, which asked respondents to rate different policy issues in their importance for the vote. The results of these polls in turn fed back into the media, further reinforcing the idea that the central criterion in deciding how to vote was policy. Moreover, as will be seen in chapter 2, this frame was not new in the case of the 2014 referendum and had a history in previous discourses around Scottish independence.

Similarly, although personal deliberations with others may be a moderating factor in whether an individual will adopt a frame (Druckman, 2001, 2004), the interlocutors in these conversations are also exposed to and possibly influenced in what they say to each other by media frames. This deliberation with others, as a moderating element, does not take place in a vacuum but may potentially draw on frames that originated in other parts of the public sphere, outside the interpersonal conversation. Media are key platforms where citizens access information about politics and as such the frames that they use are significant in shaping the ways available to think about an issue. Even though the media may not 'brainwash' individuals into adopting frames, they perform an important role in shaping the available options and definitions among which citizens choose the frames they adopt.

The next section will discuss some of these ways to think about political events which the media make available, particularly relating to how political contests like elections and referendums are commonly framed in the news.

Framing politics as policy and game

The way the media cover election campaigns has attracted ongoing scholarly attention starting as early as the 1940s (Patterson, 1980) and remains a key area of enquiry in political communication. Much of this research has sought to establish media influences on voting – even early media effects theories, long before framing, relied on evidence from election campaigns (see Williams, 2003, for a discussion of different approaches to media effects). As mentioned in the previous section, framing effects research has also offered useful insights into how voters use media content in making political decisions.

However this book will not focus on the effects of campaign framing on voting but on a previous step of the framing process: how frames are created or selected for inclusion in the media in the context of a political campaign. Although specific election or referendum campaigns will give rise to individual, issue-specific frames, the *strategic game* and *policy* frames are two frames that have been identified in the coverage of elections across different national and political contexts. Because of their broad applicability, they are 'generic' frames, namely identifiable in the coverage of different topics and in different contexts (de Vreese, 2012). The *strategic game* frame constructs an election, a referendum or a political debate more broadly as a competition or game of strategy between political opponents. It focuses on who is winning and who is losing the 'race', it analyses candidates' performance, style and perception, it involves war and game metaphors and references to opinion polls, in order to measure how opponents are doing in the competition (Patterson, 1993; Cappella and Jamieson, 1997). The issue frame, by contrast, focuses on policy problems, politicians' proposals for their resolution and their implications for the public (Lawrence, 2000).

The two frames are seen as contrasting ways of understanding politics, with the *issue* frame associated with substantive debate of policy (Lawrence, 2000) and the *game* frame commonly perceived as contributing to disengaged and cynical citizens (Cappella and Jamieson, 1997). Both the normative approaches to the role of the media in democracy, which were outlined earlier in this chapter, view the *game* frame as potentially harmful to democracy, albeit to different degrees: from the perspective of the participatory approach, the *game* frame is deplorable because it posits ordinary citizens as spectators of politics, rather than as participants; because it does not provide people with necessary information about the issues at stake; and because it encourages cynicism and distrust towards politics; from the perspective of the liberal approach, only the second of the above points is problematic (the *game* frame does not allow enough focus on political issues) since this approach does not encourage any more active engagement of citizens with politics than voting for their preferred political proposals (Strömbäck, 2005).

Therefore many authors, implicitly adopting these normative expectations on journalism, discuss the *issue* frame as being 'better' for informed citizenry and democratic debate focusing people's attention on the 'substance' of the political process (Lawrence, 2000). Others, on the other hand, propose that audiences in fact prefer watching *game*-framed to *issue*-focused media coverage (Iyengar *et al.*, 2004), which may suggest that the former is more successful in attracting attention to politics. Arguably a negative view of the *game* frame reflects an understanding of political decision-making as primarily a rational rather than an emotional process, where arguments on policy have a higher status than the horserace of the campaign. The latter may stir emotions of excitement, worry or anger, it may link the electoral decision with whether a politician's performance resonates emotionally with voters, but it is seen as a less productive way of approaching political issues because it does not promote logical evaluation of political proposals. By contrast, other scholars suggest that political thought and action do also have an emotive aspect, which co-exists with the rational one and it is not as simple to untangle them (Verstraeten, 1996; Dahlgren, 2006). As I will propose in chapter 4, the *issue* and *game* frames may in fact be complementary rather than contrastive, as they represent two facets of a political campaign that – for better or for worse – are both essential in how voters make their choices.

Due to its negative normative associations explained directly above, the *game* frame has attracted a lot of scholarly attention, with a range of authors having sought patterns for when this frame may appear in news content. One of the most commonly cited patterns is that the *game* frame tends to be used more in commercial than in public service media organisations (Strömbäck and van Aelst, 2010; Dimitrova and Strömbäck, 2011), although both types of media resort to it when a political competition is tight (Dunaway and Lawrence, 2015). It has also been found to appear more often around the period when an actual decision has to be made and conflict between elites culminates, rather than at the early stages of a debate when the *issue* frame is more prominent (Lawrence, 2000). In a comprehensive review of literature on the *game* frame, Aalberg *et al.* (2012) propose that it reflects modern campaigning which has become increasingly strategic; it is connected to the wide availability of opinion polling; it satisfies newsworthiness criteria with its focus on drama, conflict and elite actors; and it provides a way for journalists to protect their autonomy against political spin.

The above insights mostly derive from studies measuring the occurrence of the *game* frame as a dependent variable in news coverage of elections, in relation to independent variables such as proximity to the election day or the (public or private) ownership status of the news medium. Other suggestions (for example that it protects journalistic autonomy) are assumptions made by scholars to explain the prominence of the *game* frame. Nonetheless, the above debate around the *game* frame clearly tells us that this is a 'journalistic' frame, created by conditions that depend on the media rather than on their sources. The frames journalists introduce in the news are usually not advocacy frames, but are rather 'more apparent in playing-up, neglecting or juxtaposing advocacy frames' (de Vreese, 2012: 367). They are less about substance and more about process (de Vreese, 2012: 368).

However, empirical research so far has not focused equally on how journalists themselves experience the *game* and *issue* frames and why they think they give prominence to them in their accounts. As mentioned earlier in this chapter, researchers have delivered significant insights into the frame-building process from the point of view of journalists in different contexts either more generally or with reference to issue-specific frames (Kothari, 2010; Castelló and Montagut, 2011; Boesman *et al.*, 2015; Tandoc, 2015). Just one study (Bartholomé *et al.*, 2015) has particularly concentrated its attention on a generic frame, looking at how the *conflict* frame emerges in the news based on the perspectives of Dutch journalists. In their interviews with journalists on their use of the *conflict* frame, Bartholomé *et al.* (2015) found that journalists' perception of their own role as trustworthy reporters of 'facts' limits the extent to which they introduce (or admit to introducing) *conflict* frames in the news. On the other hand, factors that promote the use of the *conflict* frame include the norm of objectivity, which requires journalists to juxtapose opposing perspectives in every story; the attractiveness of the conflict frame as a narrative structure that fulfils criteria of newsworthiness; while conflict tends to be amplified more in media reports when it is between powerful, high-profile actors and when it is likely to have implications for policy. Therefore factors at the individual, professional routines and extra-media levels (Shoemaker and Reese, 2014) play a role in journalists' adoption of *conflict* frames.

Although conflict is not originally a component of the *strategic game* frame, it has often been associated with it because the latter's 'focus on metaphors from wars, games and competition did suggest that the *game* frame was inherently conflictual in nature' (Pedersen, 2014: 902). Despite this similarity though, the two frames are conceptually distinct: according to Pedersen (2014) news that contains the *strategic game* frame does not necessarily emphasise political conflict and negative campaigning (although the reverse is often the case).

Aalberg *et al.* (2012: 173) point out that although research shows that the *game* frame has become a very important feature of news around the world, 'the level of such framing and the conditions under which they are most likely to occur remains to be comprehensively investigated'. Chapter 6 addresses this question by exploring the factors that may give rise to the *strategic game* frame based on journalists' accounts of their coverage of the 2014 Scottish referendum, while chapter 6 discusses these findings in relation to what we know about the frame in other national contexts. Chapter 6 also proposes a frame-building model to explain the presence of this frame in the coverage of referendum campaigns more generally.

The same chapters also explore which factors may encourage the prominence of the *issue* frame in news coverage. In contrast to the *game* frame, *issue* or 'substantive' frames are introduced into public discourse by social and political actors, especially in the context of referendums (Hanggli and Kriesi, 2010: 154), to construct events in ways that favour their own positions. Journalists, however, retain control over the space they allow to source frames in the media – data from interviews with the journalists that covered the 2014 referendum will be analysed in chapter 5 to discuss what factors may allow some source frames to become more prominent than others.

Both *issue* and *game* frames commonly emerge in the news coverage of most elections and referendums, although they are by no means limited to these contexts. The *strategic game* frame was in fact originally conceptualised in studies of election coverage (Patterson, 1993; Cappella and Jamieson, 1997). Although, as mentioned earlier, much literature views the *game* frame as detracting attention from serious deliberation on substance, it has been found to attract voters' interest in the political process more effectively than the issue frame (Iyengar *et al.*, 2004), while its focus on opinion polls can be particularly useful for undecided voters who are trying to make up their minds near the election date (Irwin and Van Holsteyn, 2008). Although the *game* frame is commonly accused of causing cynicism and disengagement with the electoral process (Cappella and Jamieson, 1997), empirical evidence does not always support this hypothesis (de Vreese and Semetko, 2002).

Engagement with the political process is perhaps even more important in the case of referendums, since the decisions made are often one-off opportunities to settle a specific issue and every individual vote counts for the final outcome. The next section will discuss work that specifically explores the media framing of referendum campaigns. As will be seen, despite their differences from election campaigns, the media coverage of these two types of event shares many of the same frames.

Framing referendum campaigns in the media

Referendums provide a more complex environment for the media to report in than regular elections. They are much less regular compared to elections and their purpose is not to elect political representatives but to allow the electorate to make a (usually) one-off decision on a single divisive matter. Political parties may be split over the referendum issue or they may come together in unexpected coalitions to support one of the proposed options (de Vreese and Semetko, 2004). Public opinion is particularly volatile in referendums (LeDuc, 2002) and party partisanship does not predict how people will vote – although the popularity of the politicians who propose the referendum sometimes does (LeDuc, 2002). Referendum issues are often 'multi-faceted and different aspects may trigger diverse perceptions of the issue among voters' (de Vreese and Semetko, 2004: 1). Therefore, how the referendum issue is framed in the media is particularly important in this type of political event, perhaps even more so than in elections.

How one defines what the referendum issue is about has implications for what voting one way or the other will mean and, as seen earlier in this chapter, the news media have a key role in placing different definitions in the public sphere for consideration by the electorate. Yet perhaps due to the relative uncommonness of referendums, relatively few studies have so far looked at the framing of referendums in the media. These will be reviewed directly below.

Robinson (1998) examined the news coverage of the 1980 Quebec referendum for independence and found that the media primarily framed the referendum as a *strategic game* between two sides, and not as a matter of policies, nor as a citizen consultation. She suggests that the dominance of the *game* frame in previous Canadian election campaigns also 'coloured' the referendum coverage, that the binary nature of the decision allowed journalists to simplify the debate into two opposing camps and shifted attention away from the substance of the issue voted on to the contest and strategic competition between politicians. Like Cappella and Jamieson (1997) – the authors who originally conceptualised the *game* frame – Robinson is also pessimistic about its potential to contribute to democratic decision-making.

De Vreese and Semetko's (2002, 2004) study of the 2000 Danish referendum on the adoption of the euro found both strategy and issue frames in the media coverage. The *strategic game* frame was present in up to 69 per cent of the coverage they studied on different media platforms and, although it did contribute to voter cynicism, de Vreese and Semetko found that it did not have a detrimental effect on voter turnout and mobilisation, as they suggest that 'voters may be dissatisfied, cynical, and negative but still mobilized and sufficiently engaged to turn out to vote' (2002: 632). They also found in their analysis that, within their issue framing, the competing campaigns emphasised different aspects, some of which were not directly in the jurisdiction of the referendum but politicians were successful in indirectly associating them with emotional aspects of the topic. These issues were more successful in resonating with the media. They also discovered that exposure to mediated information in the final stages of the referendum campaign crystallised voters' decisions on how to vote and that public understanding of the referendum issue was influenced by the media (2004).

Gerth and Siegert (2012), on the other hand, did not explore horserace framing in their study of media coverage of the Swiss 2008 popular initiative on the naturalisation of immigrants. Instead they identified three main issue-specific frames, which originated in the discourses of the political campaign camps. They concluded that journalists simply accepted and reproduced elite frames, without developing their own arguments. This was partly because journalists routinely followed the news conferences and public appearances of political actors and adopted frames through these interactions. In the same case study, Hanggli and Kriesi (2010, 2012) also found a high dependence of journalistic framing on political actors. They proposed that although frame-building is the result of interaction between political elites and journalists, the former usually take the lead. They found that political actors introduced all the substantive frames identified in the media during that campaign, countered the frames of their adversaries, and journalists interfered very little in frame-building by comparison, although they did seem to introduce contest frames more than their sources did. Based on this premise that elite political sources, rather than journalists, are the primary frame-builders in the media, Hanggli (2012) analyses the content of campaign material produced by political actors and the media coverage during the same Swiss campaign, and argues that the key determining factor for whether a frame will be present in the media is the level of power of the political source that promotes it, while the frequency with which it will appear depends on how often the specific frame is promoted by political elites. The news media, according to the same study, have little agency and just reproduce faithfully the framing of politicians.

The Swiss studies above confirm a position initially advanced by Hall *et al.* (1978), which argues that powerful elite politicians enjoy a primary definer role in the news. According to this thesis, the routine processes of newsgathering privilege the perspectives of the powerful, because journalists, in their quest for credible, reliable sources who carry recognised authority, turn to elite sources first. Of course news reports may also include other sources but, according to this thesis, the perspective of political elites has a primary position and gets to frame the entire debate. Others questioned this account by suggesting that the news is a field where 'competition for access' takes place between different social groups and where there are opportunities for the views of the less privileged to define public debate (Schlesinger, 1990). Schlesinger argues that becoming a primary definer is a result of 'successful strategic action' (1990: 77) in putting messages across, which is often, though not necessarily or exclusively, achieved by powerful sources. Indeed framing is a power struggle among different elite groups, as well as elite and non-elite sources, and between sources and journalists.

A view that sees journalists simply as passive 'senders' of their sources' frames delivers a one-dimensional, black-and-white account of the framing process. As discussed earlier in this chapter a range of internal or external factors to the media may push journalists towards one of two ends of a frame-setting–frame-sending continuum (Brüggemann, 2014). Understanding the frame-building process as a continuum allows for a more nuanced account to help explain to what extent and why journalists may intervene to 'reframe' (Castelló and Montagut, 2011) their sources' frames while also reproducing them.

Media framing and the 2014 Scottish referendum

This is precisely the perspective this book takes to frame-building – drawing on evidence from media coverage and interviews with those directly involved in creating this coverage, the present study seeks to understand what factors may have contributed to certain frames becoming more prominent than others in the media accounts. The Scottish referendum context is distinct from the ones discussed in the previous section in many ways: the UK's media system is different from that of Switzerland or Denmark (Hallin and Mancini, 2004); the topic of Scottish the referendum is comparable (although certainly not identical) to that in Quebec, but it is different from the topics in the other referendums just discussed; the historical circumstances that led to the referendum are different in the Scottish case; as is the degree to which the referendum issue had been considered by the public prior to the campaign. The length of the campaign was also unusually long in the Scottish case.

Yet, as will be seen in subsequent chapters, there is much that frame-building in the Scottish referendum shares with that in the other contexts reviewed above. Like elsewhere, the Scottish campaign was highly divisive and contentious. Broadcasters were bound by rules of impartiality, which brought them under severe public scrutiny; newspapers were partisan, and all but one chose to support the No side. The referendum was at the time seen as a one-off decision on the issue, although this might prove not to be the case in future years. The Yes and No camps were made up of coalitions of parties with differing size, power and ideology. Strategic communications campaigns were put together on both sides and put pressure on journalists to get their frames into the news. The way that journalists worked in their day-to-day coverage of the campaign had an impact on the frames that became prominent in the public sphere. Studying journalists' perspectives can reveal much about how the dynamics of referendum campaigns may lead to specific types of frames.

Before I examine these processes in detail in chapters 3 and 5, chapter 2 will look at the Scottish context specifically and explain how the proposal for a referendum on Scottish independence emerged historically in the first place, and the role of nationalism in Scotland's relationship with the British union. I will look at the political and media environment in which the 2014 referendum took place, and how the two campaigns were formed. The chapter will also discuss the way the referendum question was phrased and the status of public opinion on the issue. The next chapter willl thus provide useful background context in which to understand the frames that the two sides of the campaign decided to promote, which will then be presented in chapter 3.

2

The Scottish constitutional issue and the 2014 referendum

Insofar as democratic politics can ever influence social change, it probably does so through a dialectic of this sort – radical pressure, slow establishment response, compromise that leads to disillusion among the radicals, and then in turn the next round of pressure. (Paterson, 2015: 27)

The 2014 Scottish referendum was the first time the Scottish electorate had the opportunity to decide whether the nation would stay in the United Kingdom or become an independent country. It was the result of a long historical process that developed particularly during the second half of the twentieth century, through which Scotland became increasingly distant from the British union and its centre of power at Westminster (Jones, 1997; McCrone and Lewis, 1999; Denver, 2002). A number of factors contributed to this, including the economic challenges faced by the formerly powerful and prosperous British state and its shift from a primarily industrial to a service-based economy, which accentuated inequalities between the north and the south of the UK; the long period of peace which no longer required the nations of the UK to unite against an external enemy; the series of Conservative administrations in the 1980s which were unpopular in Scotland and were widely perceived as hostile to the nation's interests; and the gradual weakening of the Labour Party in Scotland and in England which left a gap in the political spectrum in the early 2010s that was filled differently in each nation.

The aim of this chapter is to show that discourses and frames that emerged in 2014 did not appear in a vacuum but had historical roots in the past or, in other words, were culturally resonant. Although the 2014 referendum was the first on independence, two referendums on devolution had preceded it, the second of which led to the establishment of the devolved Scottish parliament in 1999 and opened up a new stage in the political development of Scotland. This chapter will discuss all these historical processes and briefly summarise key points in

Scotland's relationship with the UK from the establishment of the union until the 2014 referendum, without which the referendum would not have happened.

Paterson (2015) proposes that Scotland's relationship with the UK had always followed a process whereby social forces in Scotland became apprehensive, believing that the nation was not treated on equal terms with the rest of the country. This frustration, according to his argument, led to a climax (in the present case the independence referendum, but the two previous devolution referendums were also such climaxes), which forced the London establishment to respond by ceding a certain degree of power to Scotland, but not enough to fully satisfy its demands. This was usually enough to appease radical forces for a while, until pressure for reform built up again.

Paterson believes that the 2014 Scottish referendum was one episode in this scenario that has defined Scotland's position in the UK, and that the same process had happened before and will be repeated in the future. He also suggests that the disputes between Scotland and London that led to 'solutions' like the referendum were never really about the constitutional structure of the UK, as might at first appear, but about disagreement on policy or a sense that Scotland was being treated unfairly in policy terms. Understanding the 2014 referendum in this way provides a useful point of departure for understanding the media frames that emerged during the campaign.

The question on the referendum ballot paper was a binary one: 'Should Scotland be an independent country?' The question itself did not include a preferred interpretation, or frame, regarding the grounds on which the decision was to be made. A decision on whether a nation should be an independent state could, for instance, be made based on its members' sense of national identity, or on a principle of democratic self-determination. As will be seen in subsequent chapters both these understandings of what was at stake were part of the framing of the Scottish referendum, but they were not the most dominant frames in the media.

This chapter proposes that the frames that the two sides of the debate promoted instead (and which in turn impacted on the frames that were found in the media coverage of the campaign, as will be seen in later chapters) had partly to do with the historical events that led up to the point that Scotland officially considered national sovereignty from the UK in 2014. This chapter discusses these events and provides the context within which the frames that will be analysed in chapters 3, 4 and 5 may be located and understood.

Scotland in the United Kingdom and devolution

Scotland's relationship with its British neighbours, and particularly with England, was shaped over many centuries. The wars with England before the union, the growth and decline of the British empire and industrial economy, the relevant civic autonomy Scotland maintained after joining the United Kingdom, the rise of Scottish nationalism in the twentieth century, and the political developments in the second half of the twentieth century all played an important role in this relationship and eventually led to devolution in 1997; while the developments in the early post-devolution years paved the way for the referendum in 2014.

This section provides a brief overview of these events and argues that pragmatic considerations, were important in shaping Scotland's relationship with England and the UK. This is significant in understanding how the 2014 independence referendum was framed and may partly help explain why – as will be seen in chapter 3 – symbolic frames were relatively marginal in the media debate.

In the eleventh century, a small, centralised Scottish state was created within the undefined Scottish territory and began to succeed in controlling, variously, foreign invaders, local barons and warlords, and Highland clans. Wars against English invaders were common and helped strengthen and shape a Scottish sense of distinctiveness from the English 'enemy', for example as evidenced in the 1320 Declaration of Arbroath. When much later, from 1603, the Stuart dynasty ruled both the Scottish and English kingdoms, this Scottish distinctiveness persisted and was evident in the fact that two nations maintained separate parliaments. In the seventeenth century there were many unsuccessful efforts to unite the two countries.

The Act of Union came in the early eighteenth century as a proposal put forward by England to merge England and Scotland under a common political authority. At the time, Scotland was an agricultural economy facing difficulties in competing in international trade. Poor harvests in the 1690s increased death rates and emigration from the region, while war against France and Spain (in which Scotland took part with England as part of the same kingdom) increased economic strain. This became even worse after a failed Scottish expedition to set up a colony in Central America hoping to establish trade activity in the area.

At the same time there was a sense in Scotland that King James VI did not have Scottish interests at heart. Scotland was not consulted about going to war or about succession plans on who would be the next king. This led to resentment in Scotland and the passing of parliamentary acts in 1703–4 that the English saw as hostile (Devine, 2016). Already before the two nations were politically united, a pattern was becoming established of Scots feeling that they were treated unfairly when governance decisions were made.

The English saw in the idea of uniting the two nations a potential solution to give them more control over Scotland and thus they proposed an agreement between the two parliaments to 'safeguard national security ... dissolve the Edinburgh parliament and create new legislature' (Devine, 2016: 19). Scotland would become part of a state ruled by the parliament in London, where Scotland would also be represented, and it would receive economic benefits including free access to English and international markets.

The Church of Scotland and some Scottish regions were initially opposed and there were other demographic differences in response. Popular anti-union demonstrations took place in Glasgow and Edinburgh, but inside the Scottish parliament the pro-union side was powerful while opposition was split. After some negotiations, the Scottish parliament agreed, and the Act was passed on 16 January 1707 by 110 votes to 67. The fact that Scotland agreed to become part of the union, and was not occupied in war, has always made the union appear like a – impermanent – choice (McCrone, 2001).

In the early years there was some resistance to the union, particularly when unpopular measures were taken by the London government in the areas of religion and taxation. These objections eventually decreased, as the benefits from being in the United Kingdom became more material (Devine, 2016).

The two nations were connected by their geographical closeness, their majority protestant identity as opposed to Catholic areas of mainland Europe and a common front in war against other European countries. Other important advantages from joining England in a union were the financial advantages Scotland would acquire through the British empire, British industrialisation and commerce (Colley, 1992; Guibernau and Goldblatt, 2000; McCrone, 2000; Devine, 2016).

At the same time though, Scotland retained a considerable degree of civil autonomy within the British state and had a 'semi-detached' status within the union (Brown et al., 1998; McCrone, 2000, 2001), while conflict with Westminster was managed and negotiated. This was possible because Scotland maintained three important independent institutions: the Scottish law and judicial system, the Church of Scotland and the Scottish education system (Devine, 1999; Guibernau and Goldblatt, 2000; McCrone, 2000). There was thus a complex interaction between these institutional structures and the maintenance of Scottish cultural difference and distinctiveness.

Moreover, the Scottish Office, established in 1885, provided a means for bureaucratic self-government (McCrone, 2000; Schlesinger *et al.*, 2001), which allowed to defuse potential sources of friction with Westminster. According to Kumar (2003: 8), there was 'a distinctive Scottish civil society ... that could make many Scots feel that the union with England was provisional', while 'the real business of running Scotland remained the responsibility of Scots and institutions inherited from the period before 1707' (Devine, 2016: 39). This sense that the union was provisional and that Scotland was semi-autonomous within the UK was maintained throughout its history in the union although for a very long time it did not lead to its contestation.

Since 1707, Scotland has been a 'stateless nation' (McCrone, 2001) within the state structure of the UK. A nation-state combines the institutions, 'internal uniformity of rule' and political authority over a territory that characterise a state, with a culture, history and values shared by a people who belong to a nation (Guibernau and Goldblatt, 2000: 124). Scotland is a stateless nation because it has the latter but not all the aspects of the former. Nation-states as units in which the world is organised are widely considered as a sociological rather than a geographic construct, and a relatively recent one as well. Many scholars (Anderson, 1983; Balibar, 1991; Wallerstein, 1991, among others) believe that capitalism was one of the factors that gave rise to the nation-state form as we know it today. The boundaries between nations are not primarily spatial borders but sociological ones, which are defined with reference to space (Simmel, 1997: 143).

For over two centuries, the union delivered financial benefits for Scotland, providing access to new markets and opportunities for economic growth (Kidd, 1997). Increasing industrialisation in Scotland led over time to Glasgow becoming a major manufacturing city. Free trade within the UK and the rest of the British empire allowed the growth of Scottish exports, particularly in linen and tobacco. Guibernau and Goldblatt (2000) point out that by the end of the nineteenth century Scotland had turned into one of the most industrialised and advanced economies. They argue that the prosperity and civic autonomy that Scotland enjoyed at the time overshadowed its differences with England and kept Scotland largely content within the union. Besides, Scotland enjoyed adequate representation in the British parliament, while British public expenditure was favourable for the region. Indeed, the British state was more a political and financial union than a proper nation with substantial historical or identity bonds (Brockliss and Eastwood, 1997; Taylor, 2000). Scottish middle classes benefited from it, and by the Victorian times it had become 'the unquestioned sheet anchor of the

Scottish economic miracle' (Devine, 2016: 50) to which middle-class Scots attributed their prosperity. Moreover, Scots saw themselves as equal partners with England in the success of the British empire. This narrative guaranteed the union's continued stability.

One of the early signs of organised Scottish nationalism was the establishment of the National Association for the Vindication of Scottish Rights in 1853, a movement that lasted only three years. The Association never contested the union itself, but expressed disdain concerning Scotland's position within it (Kidd, 1997).

Nationalism is the political movement proposing that a nation cannot be complete unless it becomes a nation-state (Gellner, 1983; Breuilly, 1985). When a nation is already a nation-state, the role of nationalism is to express and promote national identity (Wallerstein, 1991), which over time helps maintain the state structure by reproducing an ideology of belonging. Billig (1995, 2009) distinguishes between the 'hot', openly expressed and easily identifiable organised nationalism, which is expressed by political initiatives claiming national status, demonstrations, referendums or even wars; and its 'banal', unnoticed version, which permeates everyday life in well-established nation-states. In the Scottish case, hot nationalism took a long time to gain ground.

Nairn (1977) argues that in the eighteenth and nineteenth centuries, when nationalism emerged in many European countries, Scotland failed to develop its own nationalism due to the prosperity it enjoyed within the union. According to this argument, the middle classes and the intelligentsia did not face the need to generate a nationalist ideology and this 'essential step' in the progress of a country towards modernity was delayed. When Scottish nationalism did emerge in the twentieth century, it was because the financial benefits of the union ceased and a political rather than a cultural type of nationalism emerged (Nairn, 1977). The idea that the emergence of Scottish nationalism was based on political rather than cultural and symbolic arguments is something other authors agree on, even if they don't share Nairn's conviction about the unusualness of the Scottish case.

For example, Hearn (2012) suggests that conflict around patterns of authority is commonly triggered by a politicisation of issues that were formerly taken for granted, like health, education or the distribution of wealth. This process, which also gave rise to twentieth-century Scottish nationalism in the form of a questioning of London's authority over policy-making in Scotland, is not only characteristic of the Scottish case, according to Hearn, but has also led to questioning power structures in other contexts.

The history of formal Scottish nationalism though is primarily connected with the emergence and growth of the Scottish National Party (SNP). This was first established in 1934, with the merging of the National Party of Scotland (established in 1928) and the Scottish Party (established in 1932). Initially the SNP attracted a small right-wing, rural electorate. Its positions were strongly nationalistic, supporting complete separation from the union. Devine (2016) argues that the party in its early years failed to capitalise on the financial anxiety of the electorate during the Great Depression because it proposed no convincing alternative strategy. When the Second World War started, the issue of Scottish independence completely fell off the agenda as Britain fought united against an external enemy.

In the following decades, though, things changed: Britain gradually lost its colonies; the manufacturing sector, which was a major source of prosperity for Scotland, started to decline internationally and was replaced by a growing services sector; poverty and unemployment rose in Scotland; globalisation increased the need for new narratives of local identity; a long period of relative peace after the Second World War meant that the nations of the United Kingdom no longer had to fight wars together; and the oil discovered in the North Sea between 1969 and 1971 renewed confidence in Scotland's financial potential. Many historians see these changes as having eventually enabled the expansion of Scottish nationalism.

Arguably, just like the factors that led Scotland into the union, the aspects that contributed to the weakening of the union were also pragmatic. Considerations, like the ones mentioned above, relating to the nation's financial and political interests reinforced a sense of national distinctiveness. As Scotland gradually became less affluent than before, a sense of unfairness grew – a perception that Scotland was being treated unfairly in policy terms, or that it was unable to influence the centres of power in London (Paterson, 2015).

One of the early proponents of devolution, Tom Johnston, who was Secretary of State from 1941, argued that 'Scotland was neglected by government in London and that the signs of indifference were plain to see in the inter-war collapse of Scottish economy' (Devine, 2016: 113). He believed that devolution of powers to Scotland was necessary because Westminster did not have enough time to deal efficiently with Scottish issues. In fact, after an unsuccessful attempt by the Covenant movement – a non-partisan group of civic society actors – to secure civil independence for Scotland in 1949, the issue of Scottish autonomy never moved from the political agenda.

Devine (2016) proposes that the weakening of the union in the second half of the twentieth century was not so much due to the loss of the British empire, but to the reduced role of Britain in the world, particularly in terms of economic prominence. As manufacturing declined, Scotland and Britain lost their strong economic position and the United States become the greatest international power. Post-war Labour governments made significant investment in public services and welfare for all but eventually, to balance the budget, they restricted wages and increased taxation. People had come to expect better living standards during peacetime and expected governments to deliver them, so they were more disappointed than previous generations when their expectations did not materialise.

In Scotland this disappointment gave a boost to the SNP, which by that time was better organised. In the second half of the twentieth century, the SNP was able to 'reinvent itself and its notion of Scottish nationalism' and to expand to more progressive, middle-class voters (Guibernau and Goldblatt, 2000: 144). McCrone suggests that 'the SNP was in the right place at the right time, providing a political alternative ... when the British settlement began to fail' (2001: 25). It was thus well placed to take advantage of the decline in Scotland first of the Conservative Party, which gradually became seen as a 'remote, Anglicized elite' (Devine, 2016: 152), and later of the Labour Party in the post-devolution years, as will be seen later in this section.

After winning its first Westminster seat in a 1967 by-election in Hamilton, the SNP gradually acquired a small share of parliamentary seats: in the 1974 election it won seven seats and thereafter always polled above 10 per cent of the Scottish vote (Winetrobe and Hazell, 2005; Johns and Mitchell, 2016). The discovery of oil in the North Sea, off the coast of Aberdeen, in the late 1960s also contributed to the SNP's argument that Scotland would be financially viable outside the British union, and 'triggered voters to reflect on the divergence of the interests of Scotland from those of the UK government' (Johns and Mitchell, 2016: 8).

In the decades that followed, the SNP became a permanent part of the political scene in Scotland, even though it did not become a central actor in this scene until after devolution, in the 2000s. As will be discussed later in this section, SNP voters did not always vote for the party because they supported independence. Still the debate on Scotland's constitutional status that eventually led to the 2014 independence referendum remained in the background of political life throughout this intervening time (Mitchell, 2016a).

Jones (1992) argues that the SNP, in contrast to all other parties, was not interested in gaining a majority at Westminster. Its purpose had always been to attract attention to and within Scotland and its relative electoral success in the late 1960s and 1970s, despite being erratic, managed to achieve that, primarily by worrying its political opponents. As Schlesinger *et al.* (2001) observe, the Labour Party embraced the idea of devolution, despite being internally split about it, because it saw it as a way to stop nationalism and keep its Scottish seats, which had always been important for Labour in winning Westminster elections. 'Playing the national card' also helped Labour gain ground against the Conservative Party, which until 1966 had campaigned as the Unionist Party in Scotland (McCrone, 2001). The Conservatives' support on the other hand gradually declined. According to Devine (1999), the Conservatives stood for Protestantism, Unionism and imperial identity, but these ideas had lost their appeal in Scotland. Jones claims that the party's pre-1966 unionist ideology was more effective because it managed to respect Scottish sensitivities by 'keeping the constitutional question under constant review' (1992: 377).

Faced with competition by the SNP, internal pressure by pro-devolution backbenchers, as well as the opportunity to gain voters from the Conservative Party, Labour proposed the Scotland Act in the mid-1970s, which would establish a Scottish Assembly responsible for most issues affecting life in Scotland, but without tax-raising authority. After its election, the Labour government held a referendum on this proposal on 1 March 1979. At the time however, the Labour Party was weak and divided on the constitutional issue. Labour MP George Cunningham proposed and passed a condition that 40 per cent of the Scottish electorate would need to vote 'yes' in the referendum for devolution to happen. Although 51.6 per cent of the people who turned out voted 'yes', the overall percentage (32.9 per cent of the electorate) did not reach the required 40 per cent and no change was implemented.

During this first Scottish devolution referendum, the electorate was preoccupied with rising unemployment, industrial relations and the government's pay norms. Major strikes were taking place against the government's policies and trust in Labour had declined. The proposed powers for the new Assembly in the Scotland Act had also been compromised since its initial draft. The pro-devolution campaign, supported by Labour and the SNP (even though there were members in both parties who were against it) was not as well-resourced as the anti-devolution campaign. In addition, Scottish business and industry communities were not convinced of the merits of devolution and were concerned that it would 'raise taxes, endanger industry, produce yet more bureaucracy and increase the danger of conflict with London, at a time of mounting economic difficulty' (Devine, 1999: 590). Following the failure to establish a devolved Assembly, the SNP experienced a dramatic decline of support in the next election.

The story, however, was far from over. Disaffection in Scotland caused by UK government policies was once again a key factor that revived debate on Scottish autonomy in the 1980s and 1990s. During Margaret Thatcher's administration, Conservative government policies entailed a shift of support away from the public and manufacturing sectors, on which Scotland greatly depended. Unemployment rates rose throughout the UK and especially in northern England and Scotland. Although the decline of manufacturing had started long before the 1980s, Thatcher's deindustrialising policies precipitated a dramatically fast transformation of the economy. This meant, on the one hand, poverty and unemployment for manual workers and, on the other, an increase in low-paid, part-time service-based jobs. At the same time a more knowledge-based economy emerged, allowing social mobility and the creation of a professional society (Devine, 2016). Although the Labour Party was still popular in Scotland, this was not enough for it to win a Westminster election. The party overall was internally split and powerless, and the SNP was also going through difficult times.

The Thatcher era made the Conservative Party increasingly unpopular in Scotland, until in 1997 there was no Tory MP elected there. McCrone suggests that during the Thatcher years the Scottish Office, which was such an important part of Scottish political life, 'was on the front line of the new Right onslaught, [and] the attack on the state seemed to many to be an attack on the country itself' (2001: 106). The Conservative administration period in the 1980s and 1990s is widely seen as having enabled a 'new and stronger commitment ... in the movement for home rule, in large part as a reaction to [Thatcher's] policies' (Devine, 2016: 153).

Pragmatic considerations, relating to a perceived unfairness in how policy was implemented north of the border, were once again at the heart of the constitutional issue. In 1989, the Conservative government introduced the unpopular Community Charge (better known as the poll tax) in Scotland before England. This was an attempt to reinforce local councils, through a tax paid by all adults in their respective areas. In Scotland it was seen as an unfair measure, which disregarded differences in citizens' ability to pay, and it provoked anger and protests. Eventually the measure was dropped, but only after English MPs turned against it as well (Guibernau and Goldblatt, 2000).

The same period saw a growing perceived political disparity between Scotland and the rest of the UK. In the last quarter of the twentieth century, Labour dominated parliamentary seats in Scotland, while the Conservatives, who ruled in England, were becoming increasingly unpopular (Schlesinger *et al.*, 2001). The indigenous Scottish press gradually turned against them, accusing them of closing down traditional Scottish industries without considering the human cost. The political agenda in England and in Scotland was increasingly perceived as divergent.

Devine (2016: 182) suggests that the Conservative governments of the 1980s and 1990s destabilised the balanced partnership between Scotland and England that for many centuries had been based on 'sensitivity for Scottish interests, consultation on Scottish issues, and respect for Scotland's semi-autonomy within the Union state'. McCrone (2005a: 207) agrees that 'clever and sensitive governance', taking into consideration Scotland's particular sense of semi-autonomy, had been successful in preventing tension in the twenty-five years that followed the Second World War. However, when this approach changed, problems within the union became more pronounced. Although the process leading towards Scottish devolution had started before Thatcher's administrations and was not caused by them, these latter precipitated it by reinforcing a feeling in Scotland that it was not being heard when governance decisions were made and its interests were not taken into consideration. In other words, there was a perceived decline in the legitimacy of the UK government (Hearn, 2012: 25) and a sense that there was a democratic deficit in the way Scotland was governed.

During the 1980s, the Campaign for a Scottish Assembly (CSA) aimed to unite Labour, Liberal Democrats and the SNP, in an effort to achieve devolution in Scotland. In 1988, the CSA published its 'Claim of Right for Scotland' arguing for a separate Scottish assembly. The initiative gained the support of non-party civil society organisations, such as regional councils, trade unions, representatives of the churches, minority and women's associations, as well as members of political parties. These supporters of devolution came together in the Scottish Constitutional Convention, to create a blueprint for a Scottish parliament. Labour was at the centre of this initiative, which made it 'politically unacceptable for any future Labour government to deny the Scots a parliament' (Devine, 1999: 612). The Conservatives did not participate because they were against devolution and neither did the SNP, as they were concerned that the initiative would be dominated by Labour and that devolution would hinder rather than open the road to independence. However, there was collaboration among pro-devolution politicians from different parties, in the approach to the later referendum.

Following Labour's 1997 election victory, Tony Blair's government fulfilled the party's promise to carry out another devolution referendum. The constitutional issue had been decisive for the Scottish vote in this election (Brown *et al.*, 1998). The referendum held on 11 September 1997 concluded that there should be a Scottish parliament (74.3 per cent of the vote), with the power to vary taxation (63.5 per cent of the vote). This time the pro-devolution campaign was much stronger – the Conservatives were the only major party that campaigned against devolution. Moreover the leadership of the Labour Party was committed to achieving devolution, as opposed to the 1979 referendum. The Labour Party also enjoyed more public support in 1997 than in 1979, its views on devolution were clearer, and it was successful in persuading many middle-class Scots to vote for devolution (Evans and Trystan, 1999). The pro-devolution communication campaign was issue-driven, focusing on policy proposals such as democratising healthcare and avoiding tax rises (Jones, 1997). As will be seen in subsequent chapters, policy pledges were also central in the 2014 independence referendum.

Under the 1998 Scotland Act, the new Scottish parliament gained powers over all issues affecting daily life in Scotland, such as healthcare, education, transportation, the environment; while foreign policy, defence, national security, taxation, macro-economics, social security, abortion and broadcasting remained reserved to Westminster (Schlesinger, 1998; Murkens, 2002). The importance of this major constitutional change, according to McCrone (2001: 1), was that 'Scotland is no longer stateless'. Indeed Scotland gained some degree of state apparatus, though Westminster retained control of key areas such as foreign affairs, and, perhaps more importantly, for raising taxation and allocating the Scottish parliament its share of the state budget, based on the Barnett formula.

The brief overview of historical events examined so far lends support to the argument that tension in the nation's relationship with the British union was primarily caused by differences relating to pragmatic considerations. Both devolution referendums in 1979 and 1997 can be seen as attempts by Westminster to compromise and cede some power over policy-making in order to keep the union together, but not complete power to fully satisfy demands. In both cases pressure for Scottish independence stopped for a while, but emerged again before long, prompted once again by pragmatic factors. In both cases, behind the pressure for independence lay a perception that there was a political disparity between Scotland and Westminster and a democratic deficit in how Scotland was governed. This fed into a general sense of difference between Scottish and English society.

The fifteen years between the establishment of the first devolved Scottish parliament in 1999 and the 2014 referendum were marked by an impressive shift of the SNP to the forefront of the Scottish political scene. Devolution provided an opportunity for this to happen, because without the Scottish parliament the SNP would likely not have had the chance to get large enough numbers of Westminster MPs elected to share power, given that the Scottish vote is only one portion of the UK-wide electorate (Devine, 2016). Moreover, the SNP's support was traditionally spread throughout Scotland and this did not allow it to gain seats in the electoral system applied in Westminster elections. The new system applied in Scottish parliamentary elections allocated additional 'party list' seats according to the proportion of the vote parties achieved and this initially helped the SNP win some extra seats. In addition to that, devolution created a new, clearly distinctive Scottish political scene, which allowed more space for the SNP to gain visibility (Johns and Mitchell, 2016). That said, devolution by itself did not guarantee the SNP's rise – in fact the Scottish electoral system was set up so that a single party would not be able to easily achieve a majority and coalitions would be necessary. Devine suggests that 'the structure had been carefully designed to ensure that nationalism would never threaten the union through achieving power in Holyrood' (2016: 208).

The SNP's political success rather lies in its own strategic efforts, which gradually persuaded the Scottish electorate that it was competent and reliable in government and that it had Scotland's interests at heart, combined with the post-devolution decline of the major UK parties with Scottish branches, and particularly of Scottish Labour. The SNP built a more professional structure based on civic nationalism and a left-of-centre ideology, and it made an effort to approach demographics that had traditionally voted for Labour, such as Catholics and Muslims (Johns and Mitchell, 2016). It also invested particularly in media relations and in communicating its positions to the media, often getting the second position in share of voice in the news coverage of Scottish affairs, following Labour (Dekavalla, 2012). It thus became a major player in day-to-day Scottish politics. Throughout this early post-devolution period independence, although present, was not at the core of the SNP's political rhetoric, which focused primarily on its policy and governance proposals (McNair, 2008). This was probably meant to avoid alienating voters who were still on the whole sceptical about independence. Indeed, even after the party came to power, support for independence remained consistently below 30 per cent and stayed there well into the independence referendum debate.

The first two elections in 1999 and 2003 delivered a Labour–Liberal Democrat coalition. In the early years the devolution project and the

Scottish parliament drew negative coverage and criticism by the Scottish press. According to Winetrobe and Hazell (2005: 66), the media's 'unexpected ferocity' in covering devolution 'had a crucial negative impact on the perception (and self-perception) of the young parliament, and devolution itself'. Controversy was caused over a number of issues including the high cost of the building that housed the parliament, the decision to abolish a law prohibiting schools from 'promoting' homosexuality, infighting in the government, speculations about individual MSPs' integrity. At the same time, though, the economy was going well, the Scottish parliament took some decisions that departed from policies in England, such as providing free medical prescriptions for all patients and free personal care for the elderly, or banning smoking in public spaces before this was introduced in England. Overall the structure and procedures of the parliament meant that parliamentary committees had more power in Holyrood than in Westminster and that the parliament itself was more independent from the government (Winetrobe and Hazell, 2005). The Labour Party, which was in government both at the Scottish and the UK parliaments, ensured good co-operation between them, and support for independence was low.

On the other hand, though, the UK Labour government was becoming increasingly unpopular after the controversy over the Iraq dossiers and the Hutton Inquiry, the MPs' expenses scandal and the banking crisis. By the end of the third Labour administration at Westminster, the UK was also facing a global financial crisis. Scottish Labour was confronted by additional challenges, as part of the first two coalition governments in the Scottish parliament. There was a perception that the Scottish branch of the party was not able to take its own decisions to deal with Scotland's problems because it was too dependent on its London headquarters. It was also perceived as too confident of its electoral advantage in Scotland, as mediocre in administration when it was in power, and as not proposing new ideas, or standing up for Scotland (Devine, 2016; Johns and Mitchell, 2016).

In the longer term, a number of factors contributed to Labour's electoral decline in Scotland: trade unions, traditionally supporting Labour, experienced declining membership for many years since service sector workers are not as unionised as manufacturing workers used to be; council housing had declined and home ownership had increased; class membership no longer predicted voting patterns; large parties converged ideologically; Labour lost control in Scottish local councils following the introduction of proportional representation in local elections; the Labour Party's transformation into New Labour after 1997 did not appeal to traditional supporters who perceived it as protecting corporate interests;

the UK's participation in the Iraq war, which was initiated by Labour, was disapproved by voters (Devine, 2016; Johns and Mitchell, 2016).

Progressively Scottish voters became disillusioned with Westminster parties: first with the Conservatives and then with Labour as well. A challenge faced by UK-wide parties was how to maintain a common and consistent party line across the country, while at the same time allowing their regional branches to adapt to circumstances in their respective nations and make autonomous decisions (Trench, 2008). The SNP, on the other hand, was seen as having Scotland's interests at heart because of its *raison d'être*, but also because it was an autonomous party rather than a Scottish branch of a UK party. Through strategic planning and stable leadership, the SNP managed to win over groups of voters who were disappointed with the other parties and to fill in the gap in the left-of-centre part of the political spectrum, taking over from Labour as the most popular party in Scotland.

In 2007, the SNP won forty-seven seats against Labour's forty-six, which allowed it to form a minority government with the additional support of two Green MSPs. According to Jones (2008: 44), five factors were incremental to this first major SNP win: 'much better organization and funding, winning the votes of both "full-strength nationalists" and "nationalist-lites", a perception that it would stand up more for Scotland than Labour, having the most popular leader, and a perception that it would do a better job on devolved issues'. In its first term in office, the SNP published a White Paper on Scotland's future, which left open both the independence and the increased devolution options, followed by the launch of a 'National Conversation', whose aim was to explore the case for independence. The consultation was completed in November 2009 and led to the publication of a draft referendum bill in February 2010, however this was never voted on by the Scottish parliament. The other Scottish party leaders rejected the SNP's White Paper and proposed instead a 'Scottish Constitutional Commission' made up of experts, whose aim was to look into plans for enhancing devolution, but not to discuss independence (Jones, 2008). This led to the publication of the Calman report in June 2009, which outlined a number of further powers that should be devolved to the Scottish parliament. Its proposals were endorsed by the Labour, Conservative and Liberal Democrat parties (Mitchell, 2016a).

More importantly though, in its first electoral term the SNP was perceived as more efficient than the previous coalition governments in managing devolved issues (Devine, 2016; Johns and Mitchell, 2016). It took popular decisions, such as freezing council tax rates and abolishing tuition fees, and with its measured approach to Westminster it avoided potential conflict. This positive record played a major role in the SNP's landslide win at the 2011 Scottish elections, where it won sixty-nine of the 129 parliamentary seats. Although support for independence remained low in 2011 – much lower than the SNP's overall support, 'Scots were not voting on the constitution but on what they thought was the most able Holyrood administration and the one best suited to defend the interests of Scotland' (Devine, 2016: 221). The SNP had convinced voters that it was competent, moderate and left-of-centre (Johns and Mitchell, 2016; Mitchell, 2016a). This victory was a major achievement for the party, especially as the Scottish voting system does not easily allow for majority governments to form.

Meanwhile the Conservative-led government in London sought to face the international economic crisis with unpopular austerity policies. The contrast between a left-of-centre, nationalist government in Scotland and a right-of-centre Tory coalition at Westminster brought back narratives of a 'democratic deficit', which had dominated during the Thatcher period, and reinforced the idea that there was a disparity between Scotland and England (Devine, 2016). Westminster governments were seen as favouring the powerful – private interests, bankers and the rich – and disadvantaging the poor, for example by imposing what became known as the 'bedroom tax', a decision to restrict housing benefits for the disabled.

The SNP's win in 2011 meant that it could form a majority government and proceed with its manifesto proposal to hold a referendum on independence. Although the UK does not have a written constitution, any changes to the remit of the Westminster parliament, including devolution of powers or independence of any part of the union, have traditionally been put to the decision of the electorate through a referendum, so this kind of resolution could not be taken by parliamentary representatives alone. However, the authority to hold a referendum on the union was not within the Scottish parliament's powers and had to be negotiated and granted by the UK government (Murkens, 2002).

Soon after the SNP's election, at a time when support for independence was still low, Conservative Prime Minister David Cameron agreed for the referendum to take place. According to Devine (2016: 244) he saw the referendum as an opportunity 'to destroy the cause for "separatism" for a generation or more'. Perhaps for this reason he demanded that the question on the ballot paper was binary, for or against independence, and that it should not include the third and overall most popular option of increased devolution. Surveys early in the referendum campaign showed similar levels of support for independence, increased devolution and the status quo, while increased devolution was the 'least opposed' option (Curtice, 2014) and the one most likely to have won majority support (Mitchell, 2016a: 81; Mullen, 2016: 17). By not including it, it could be expected that Scots concerned about the uncertainty of a major change would vote for the status quo (Mitchell, 2016a). Once again the pattern discussed at the start of the chapter was repeated: pressure for more autonomy was dealt with by Westminster strategically ceding some power– in this case the opportunity to hold a referendum, but without including an option for increased devolution.

The 'Edinburgh Agreement' was signed between the Scottish and UK governments on 15 October 2012. Under the agreement, the two governments decided to work together to ensure that a referendum on Scottish independence would take place. Apart from the restriction on the options to be offered, the Scottish government was granted freedom to determine when the referendum would be held, the composition of the franchise, and the exact phrasing of the question (in consultation with the Electoral Commission). Since, as discussed earlier, support for independence was low at the time when the SNP was elected, the decision was made to have the referendum considerably later, in September 2014. It was also decided that the electorate would include everyone living in Scotland for longer than six months, even if they were not British nationals, the vote was extended to sixteen- and seventeen-year-olds, who normally did not have the right to vote in elections, but Scots who lived outside Scotland could not participate. The question was binary: Should Scotland be an independent country? This allowed the pro-independence side to defend the more positive sounding Yes option.

The two formal campaigns, designated by the Electoral Commission as representing the official pro- and anti-independence positions, were launched in mid-2012. The official Yes campaign was led by the SNP, the largest of the parties that made up the campaign, and it also included the Scottish Green Party and the Scottish Socialist Party. The Scottish Labour, Conservative and Liberal Democrat parties made up the Better Together campaign, supporting remaining in the union. Despite the party officially supporting the union, Labour voters were split over independence: a Labour for Independence group was set up by a little-known party member, but politicians did not back it (Mitchell, 2016a). Even among Labour voters who supported staying in the UK, there was discomfort with the fact that their party was campaigning alongside the Conservatives. Overall, as will be discussed in the next chapter, the No campaign had more conflicting interests internally than the Yes side.

The Yes campaign fostered a substantial grassroots movement, which was seen as having galvanised the campaign beyond what the political parties in Yes Scotland could have on their own (Paterson, 2015). According to Johns and Mitchell (2016: 198), the SNP wanted the Yes side to be seen as a separate movement, and the encouragement of grassroots campaigning was part of this strategy. The involvement of grassroots campaigners also arguably pushed both official campaigns towards a more direct engagement with voters than is usual in political campaigning. The referendum in general saw unprecedented engagement among the public, even among groups that traditionally did not participate in elections. Apart from the media debates, the issue was discussed at public meetings throughout Scotland and it was the main topic of conversation everywhere as the day of the vote approached.

The length of the campaign allowed the Yes side time to gain ground in opinion polls. In the final weeks polls showed that the two options were very close and the outcome was difficult to predict. Although all three major parties of the No campaign had previously promised that in the case of a No vote they would pursue more powers for the Scottish parliament, beyond those recommended by the Calman report, under the pressure of the final week the leaders of the Conservatives, Labour and the Liberal Democrats additionally signed a commitment on the front page of the *Daily Record* newspaper, that they would guarantee increased devolution for Scotland if the electorate voted to stay in the UK. This became known as 'the Vow' and was seen as effectively replacing the status quo option on the ballot paper with increased devolution (Johns and Mitchell, 2016; Mullen, 2016). Eventually 84.6 per cent of those registered voted, which was the highest turnout in any UK election or referendum (Barford, 2014) and voters decided that Scotland should stay in the UK (with 55 per cent support for No).

According to the ESRC Scottish Referendum Study, men, younger voters, people born in Scotland, SNP voters, working class, social housing tenants and low income voters were more likely to have voted for independence. The main reasons respondents reported for having voted Yes were 'to ensure that Scotland always gets the governments it votes for, the whole Westminster system is rotten, independence is the natural state of nations like Scotland, and Scotland would better off economically' (Mullen, 2016: 14). On the other hand, those who voted to stay in the union reported that they did so for three main reasons: 'feeling British and believing in the Union, too many unanswered questions, and a sense that independence would have made Scotland worse off economically' (Mullen, 2016: 14).

Practical considerations such as the state of the economy and Scotland's influence in political decision-making were therefore significant in voters' decision. As will be discussed in detail in the next chapter, both campaigns decided to focus on pragmatic arguments for and against independence, each for their own reasons, while national identity did not feature as much in the official campaign messages. What has become clear from the historical review in this chapter is that this was not new or specific to the 2014 referendum – pragmatic considerations had always been part of Scotland's relationship with England and the union. From the establishment of the union itself to the gradual distancing of Scotland in the 1970s and 1980s, the extent to which Scotland's economic and other policy interests would be better catered for within or outside the union always played a vital role in its relationship with Westminster. The next section will delve deeper into the argument that the basis of the differences between the two nations is pragmatic as well as, symbolic.

Scotland and national identity

Devine (2016) suggests that the survival of a distinctive Scottish identity within the union was essential in maintaining a sense that Scotland was in a partnership of equals. As explained earlier, a sense of national identity, of belonging to a group defined geographically, is an important ideology in maintaining a nation (Wallerstein, 1991). A degree of collective identification is also essential for the existence of a national public sphere: participants need to think that they share enough to have issues in common to resolve (Peters, 2008).

National identity is a perceived link between people who believe that they have a common past and a common future. Like all forms of identity it is both about 'relationships of similarity and difference' (Jenkins, 1996: 4) – this means that it is both about the links that bring a people together, but also about the features that make them distinctive from other nations. These links and characteristics are socially constituted and reproduced (Balibar, 1991; Bourdieu, 1991).

National identities are therefore 'discourses', constructed meanings, and include symbols and narratives about national histories, literatures and cultures (Hall, 1992: 292–293). National identity produces a psychological experience of belonging, even though in reality there is little homogeneity and agreement within nations about what the nation's identity is, and its definition is itself a field of struggle between different groups (Bourdieu, 1991; Billig, 2009). This is especially true in the different parts of the UK, where national identity does not have a homogeneous meaning but British and Scottish, English, Welsh or Northern Irish identities interact, sometimes contrasting and sometimes co-existing with each other.

National identity may be defined as grounded in ethnic or civic criteria of belonging. Ethnic national identities are based on the idea of a common ethnicity, of shared ancestors and history, of a shared culture and way of life (Billig *et al.*, 2005). It is what de Cillia *et al.* (1999) describe as 'Kulturnation'. Civic identities, by contrast, accept ethnic diversity within a nation and are based on citizenship and shared values, rather than on ancestry (Billig *et al.*, 2005). Modern multicultural societies require politicians to adopt a civic definition of national identity in order to appeal to as wide a spectrum of citizens as possible. If not everyone who belongs to a nation may necessarily share the same ancestry, claims to more abstract values are easier to share because committing to them is a matter of choice. Indeed, throughout the years it has been most prominent in the Scottish political scene, the SNP consistently adopted a civic form of nationalism, "refusing to be confounded with the ethnic side of nationalism that could potentially blur into chauvinism and racism" (Johns and Mitchell, 2016: 32). In fact since the 1980s ethnic notions of Scottish identity took a secondary position in SNP politics and were replaced by an emphasis on the divergence of Scottish civic values and voting behaviour (Johns and Mitchell, 2016: 53).

An important role in the process through which national identities are constructed and reproduced is held by communication in its various forms: through standardised languages, within the family, at school and in the media. Schlesinger (2000) discusses this approach as the theory of 'social communications' and traces its evolution from Deutsch in the 1950s through to Billig and Castells in the 1990s.

Deutsch (1953) and Gellner (1983) both adopt culturally based understandings of national identity, grounded on common memories and habits, which no longer seem applicable to contemporary multicultural societies. Importantly, though, they both stress the role of communication in creating national homogeneity, a view they share with Benedict Anderson. In his influential *Imagined Communities* (1983) Anderson argues that the complexity of industrial societies makes it impossible for people to have a personal experience of the entire community in which they live. The media are essential in reproducing a sense of national belonging by encouraging people over large geographical areas to imagine fellow readers, viewers or listeners simultaneously consuming the same media products.

It could be argued that Anderson's perspective is also outdated in nations which include multiple identities; that people today would no longer 'imagine' a singular community because homogeneity does not exist. Moreover media consumption is becoming increasingly fragmented, with the old media no longer commanding mass audiences watching or reading simultaneously the same news. This however does not change the fact that communication and specifically mediated communication does address audiences as communities. Such addresses may be rejected or interpreted in many ways, but Dahlgren seems to make a valid point when arguing that:

> Whether such 'communities' are 'authentic' or not is another matter, but media-based interpretive communities are a precondition for sense- making in a modern public sphere. (Dahlgren, 1991: 17)

Therefore social communication – primarily but not restricted to the media – is important in defining a public space where members of a nation debate issues of common interest with other members of the same group, and where those beyond its boundaries are seen as outsiders (Deutsch, 1953).

So how has the Scottish nation been imagined as a distinctive entity from the other nations of the UK? Surveys have long shown that for Scottish citizens civic and cultural aspects are both significant in defining Scottishness. According to one survey, 'a sense of equality, Scottish landscape, music and the arts, and the national flag' are the components Scots believe make up Scottish identity (Bechhoffer and McCrone, 2009: 14).

Although, as discussed in the previous section, it is generally agreed that Scotland maintained its distinctiveness and England did not purposefully impose on it an English way of life (Brockliss and Eastwood, 1997; Devine, 1999), there is considerable debate around what specific elements consist Scottish culture. Scottish cultural identity is often associated with the tradition and myths of the Highlands and tartanry, however, Highlandism is not an uncontested myth of Scottishness. In the early years of the union, the Highlands and their inhabitants were seen as inferior, backward and dangerous by the people of the Lowlands (Devine, 1999; Pittock, 1999). Scottish Enlightenment denounced what was then perceived as 'parochial myths of the origins of Scottish kingship and nationhood' (Devine, 2016: 75), Scottish history was not considered important during those years because the nation had a poor and turbulent past, and English parliamentary history was the main history taught.

It was only at the end of the eighteenth century that symbols of Highland tradition were used by the Scottish elite as symbols of Scottish identity. At the time, Scotland enjoyed great financial growth, but also felt threatened by cultural integration with England. Highland myths, heroes and symbols provided a much-needed identity for the rest of Scotland (Devine, 1999). Myths constructed through the nineteenth century and Kailyard novels presented Scotland as romantic, rural and free of conflict. This romantic view of the past 'provided a distinctive but inoffensive mode of differentiation from England without in any way threatening or compromising the Union' (Devine, 2016: 82).

In the twentieth century though, Highland symbols and myths were perceived as sentimental and kitsch. Tartanry was seen by scholars as preventing Scots from defining their identity (Paterson, 1981), as limiting popular consciousness (McArthur, 1981), and as sustaining a sense of passivity in Scottish society (Craig, 1982). Pittock makes a valid point when arguing that although this symbolism served as 'a most unproblematic image of Scottishness outside Scotland itself', Scots changed their views about it over time (1999: 88).

Apart from traditions and myths, there are two distinctive Scottish languages, Scots and Gaelic, which declined significantly over the centuries. Gaelic used to be widespread but gradually became limited geographically to the Highlands where it still has more speakers. Scots, originally the language of the Lowlands, functions as an overarching term for several varieties, which can be intelligible to speakers of English because they share many features with it (Corbett, 2008). Therefore it is not as easily accepted as a distinctive language as Gaelic is and there is politically driven debate on whether it is a language or a dialect. Today, Scots dialects are still spoken and function as markers of regional and social class, as well as national identity (Corbett, 2008). Although the capacity to speak Welsh is integral to national identity in Wales, in Scotland linguistic distinctiveness in itself does not necessarily 'objectify national cultural capital' (McCrone, 2005b: 73).

The above discussion suggests that although cultural, symbolic markers of Scottish identity existed within the union, for many centuries Scottishness fitted smoothly into Britishness – what Devine describes as 'banal unionism' (2016: 92) – and did not clash with it. When Scottish nationalism did emerge in the twentieth century, as seen in the previous section, it was instigated by political rather than purely cultural differences.

The idea that Scottish identity is rather civic in nature and consists in a particular set of political and social convictions is widespread. McCrone (2005b) suggests that Scottish culture does not have a single carrier, such as a uniform language, religion or ethnicity. What he believes distinguishes the Scots as a nation is a different 'cultural prism for translating social change into political meaning and action' and this is the difference in cultural capital between Scotland

and England (2005b: 79). Johns and Mitchell (2016: 54) argue that particularly during and after the Thatcher years, Scottish identity became 'a more explicitly political identity for many Scots', expressing their disagreement with a political point of view that they saw as British, rather than with a traditional sense of nationhood. This argument is in line with the view proposed at the start of this chapter, namely that pragmatic considerations and power imbalance have long fed into a sense of Scottish cultural distinctiveness within the UK, and eventually into claims to independence. The next section will look at the components of such a distinctive Scottish political identity.

Scottishness, citizenship and political change

The British National Election Survey has been carried out since 1963, before major elections, to record changes in political attitudes. The survey includes an investigation of national identity, which asks respondents to position themselves on a scale (the Moreno scale) that rates which geographical identity has priority in the way they define themselves: the regional (English, Scottish, Welsh) or the national (British). Additionally, the survey asks respondents to identify the significance their different identities (national, social class, gender, age, etc.) hold for them.

A significant finding of these surveys is that being Scottish is the primary way in which Scots define themselves, more so than age, gender, or social class (Bond, 2006; Bechhoffer and McCrone, 2009). Bechhoffer and McCrone, who have long been involved in the survey, note that 'however we define national identity ... we find that people in Scotland describe themselves in national identity terms' (2009: 19).

Regarding the criteria for someone to qualify as Scottish, being born in Scotland is consistently found to be the most significant one in these surveys, although having Scottish parents or a Scottish accent also counts for those who were not born in the country (Kiely et al., 2005; Bond 2006; Bechhoffer and McCrone, 2009). This suggests that ethnic rather than civic criteria are seen by the public as more important in defining Scottishness.

However the argument proposed at the end of the previous section that Scottish people have different perspectives or preferences in making political decisions does not always become evident in their responses to surveys. Brown et al. (1998) suggest that the factors influencing voting decisions in Scotland and the rest of the UK are equally connected to daily life issues, such as healthcare and education, while attitudes on issues of equality, liberty, taxation and welfare are similar on both sides of the border. As Curtice points out (2005: 165), 'Scotland and England

appear for the most part to share the same values and similar policy preferences'. Scotland is to a certain extent more left-of-centre than England
and more pro-European, but overall the two nations appear to agree on
most matters of governance (Curtice, 2005).

The main difference in poll responses between England and Scotland
is that Scots tend to identify more often as Scottish than as British.
However there remain people in both nations for whom Britishness co-
exists with sub-state national identification, perhaps most clearly illustrated in a statement by then SNP leader Alex Salmond in a television
interview in January 2014, where he claimed that he saw himself as
having a multi-layered identity, of which being British was also one part
(Johns and Mitchell, 2016: 27). By acknowledging Britishness alongside
Scottishness, Salmond avoided alienating voters who felt that the two
identities can be combined. In the same interview he claimed that the
independence referendum was not actually about identity – reflecting
once again the civic nature of SNP's nationalism, as explained earlier in
this chapter.

Overall the lack of 'a common commitment to a shared set of identities' appears to be a key factor separating Scotland from England
(Curtice, 2005: 169). However, there is no straightforward relationship between identifying as Scottish and support for independence, or
for individual parties (Paterson et al., 2001; Bond and Rosie, 2002,
2006). The survey findings referred to in this section seem to generally suggest that Scottish identity has very high significance for
Scots but it does not clearly correlate with particular party or policy
preferences.

This does not mean that Scottish identity does not matter. As Blain
and Hutchison (2016: 16) suggest, 'the perception of Scottish society
and its cultures as having distinctive characteristics and rights' has
been critical in the preservation of Scottish nationhood within the
British state for centuries, and ultimately is also integral to claims for
independence. Perhaps the complexity of defining this identity though,
as discussed in this chapter, may partly explain its relatively marginal position both in campaign messages and in media coverage of
the 2014 referendum, which will be discussed in subsequent chapters.
As Mitchell (2016b: 9) proposes, national identity was important in
the referendum, but it was 'refracted through everyday public policy
concerns'.

Moreover, if Scottish identity is difficult to define, British identity is
even more so. McCrone (2005a: 209) argues that 'the UK is less mis-
conceived than under-conceived, an absent-minded state, a state-nation,

rather than a nation-state. In other words, the state came after the nations' and there was no attempt to build a cohesive national identity for the UK. Similarly, Hassan suggests that the UK is a 'nationless state' (2014: 23), which perceives nationalism as a thing of the past, because Britishness, like Scottishness, is primarily a civic notion (Johns and Mitchell, 2016). Britishness in England was traditionally conflated with Englishness, which led to further confusion when traditional notions of what Britain is were contested by the collapse of the British empire, the change in Britain's international position, immigration and multiculturalism, and the gradual distancing of Scotland and Wales (Pittock, 1999; Taylor, 2000; Kumar, 2003; McCrone, 2005b).

The Scottish media

This section will focus particularly on the Scottish media landscape and the organisations that make it up. This is significant in understanding the role of news media, and particularly print and broadcast media on which this study focuses, in public debate around the 2014 Scottish referendum.

Together with the Scottish legal and judicial system, the Church of Scotland and the Scottish education system, the Scottish press is often said to have played a vital role in maintaining Scottish distinctiveness within the United Kingdom (Connell, 2003). Most of the indigenous Scottish newspapers that are in the market today (the *Scotsman*, the *Herald*, the *Daily Record*, the *Press and Journal*, the *Courier*) were established in the eighteenth and nineteenth centuries, while London titles started producing dedicated Scottish editions in the twentieth century (Hutchison, 2008). The BBC, the UK-wide public service broadcaster, started transmitting in Scotland in 1952; Scottish Television (STV) and Grampian, which were the Channel 3 licensees for Central and Northern Scotland, started in 1957 and 1961 respectively. Following the establishment of the latter two, the BBC's Scottish operation was renamed as BBC Scotland. Hassan (2014) argues that while the (indigenous) Scottish press was established to serve a mostly unionist bourgeoisie, Scottish broadcasting was set up in a period of universal suffrage and working-class emancipation after the Second World War, and although its content was never nationalist, simply the presence of dedicated Scottish broadcasters was significant in reinforcing Scottish distinctiveness.

Scottish indigenous newspapers changed ownership a number of times during their history and many of them have been or are still, at the time of writing, owned by companies outside Scotland. The *Scotsman*, for example, was part of the Canadian Thomson Group from the 1950s until the mid-1990s, was subsequently owned by the Barclay brothers and then by Scottish publishers Johnston Press, whose commercial interests and shareholders are UK-wide rather than just Scottish (Blain and Hutchison, 2016). The *Herald* is currently owned by Newsquest Plc, a subsidiary of American Gannet Corporation, to which it was sold by the Scottish Media Group in 2002. The *Daily Record* was established by Alfred Harmsworth, who later became the press baron Lord Northcliffe and who also founded the *Daily Mirror* – still in the same group as the *Record* – although the company itself was sold and is currently based in England (the Trinity Mirror Group). D.C. Thomson, one of the two most successful Scottish newspaper publishers, together with Johnston Press, owns the *Dundee Courier* and the *Aberdeen Press and Journal*.

English newspapers, like the *Sun*, the *Mirror* or the *Daily Mail*, began to target the Scottish market with separate editions from the 1970s onwards. These titles reproduce part of their content in all their editions, and some pages only are made specifically for the different regions/ nations they circulate in. With the more generous financial resources they enjoy, these London titles introduced additional rivalry in an already crowded market competing for a relatively small potential readership of just over five million. Despite the recent decline of the entire newspaper market, Scottish editions remain a major competitor for the indigenous press (Dekavalla, 2015). Indeed, in 2006 the *Scottish Sun* overtook the *Daily Record* as the best-selling title in Scotland for the first time since the 1970s (Hutchison, 2008) and has remained in this position until the time of writing.

Newspapers in the UK are openly partisan and the political orientation of Scottish newspapers has changed through time, depending on their owners, their editors but also on commercial considerations. The *Daily Record*, a traditionally Labour supporting title, occasionally opposed proposals of the Labour–Liberal Democrat Scottish Executive in the first years of devolution (Hutchison, 2008). The *Scottish Sun*, which usually follows the political alliance of its London edition, from supporting the Conservatives in the 1980s and early 1990s to Blair's New Labour in 1997, briefly supported the SNP in the 1992 general election and then again in the 2011 Scottish election, but it never adopted a pro-independence agenda. The *Herald*, once a Conservative newspaper, changed its support at the end of the twentieth century towards a more liberal position. The *Scotsman* and the *Dundee Courier* remain more right-of-centre, though neither of them support the Conservatives in the explicit way of the *Scottish Daily Mail*. In fact the *Scotsman*, the *Herald* and their Sunday editions all supported the SNP in the 2011 election, without supporting independence (Hassan, 2014). Yet, despite their differences in political views, a consensus seemed to emerge among these titles in the early devolution years, which was sceptical about Scottish independence and critical about the early performance of the Scottish parliament (McNair, 2008). During the 2014 independence referendum this translated into either outright opposition or ambivalent scepticism towards independence throughout the indigenous and editionised press, with only the *Sunday Herald* eventually coming out in favour of the Yes side.

Clearly, at the time of the referendum, and for many years before that, the press in Scotland was experiencing major decline in readership, advertising and revenue, as part of a trend that affected the press in most Western countries. In Scotland this decline was even greater due to the already overcrowded market, with sixteen daily morning titles, and several evening and weekly ones (Dekavalla, 2015). Still, the press remained a significant part of the mediated debate. Newspapers may have had a relatively restricted print readership, but they were read by political elites and by contributors to broadcast and online media, they often became themselves direct or indirect contributors to online conversations, while the material dominating the debate on 'old' media was also the main material for discussion on social media (Paterson, 2015: 23).

Television news in Scotland operates as an opt-out service from UK-wide programming. *Reporting Scotland*, BBC Scotland's daily early evening news bulletin, began in 1968. It is a half-hour programme that follows directly after the UK-wide *BBC News at Six*. STV's equivalent bulletin started in 1972, then named *Scotland Today*, and it was renamed as *STV News at Six* in 2006. By that time STV and Grampian Television had merged into one service for both regions, while the third Scottish Channel 3 licence, at the Scottish borders, was owned by ITV. Throughout its history concerns were expressed on the quality of STV's service and programming (Hassan, 2014). In 2007 its owners, the STV group, sold some of their other companies and focused on more Scottish content for STV. In the area of news and current affairs they launched a daily current affairs programme, *Scotland Tonight*, in 2011. BBC Scotland followed by replacing the Scottish edition of UK-wide current affairs programme *Newsnight* with a dedicated programme, *Scotland 2014*, during the final months of the referendum campaign and thereafter. Broadcasting rules in the UK require television and radio stations to remain impartial on all political issues and to fairly present a range of different views. This is an essential condition for maintaining their licences to broadcast and it is embedded in both the BBC's editorial guidelines (www.bbc.co.uk/editorialguidelines/) and in Ofcom's broadcasting code (Ofcom, 2013), which regulates commercial broadcasters (and as of 2017, for the BBC as well).

Throughout the devolution years there was debate about the extent to which broadcasting still served the needs of the devolved UK. In the early years of the post-devolution period there was discussion about introducing an entirely Scottish BBC evening bulletin, an idea which became known as the 'Scottish Six', to replace the BBC's offering of a central plus an opt-out half-hour programme. The idea was considered, later abandoned, returned again in 2016 but was eventually forsaken in favour of the BBC's new plans to introduce a dedicated Scottish channel with its own hour-long 9 p.m. Scottish bulletin.

The new BBC Scotland channel was announced in February 2017, and came after years of debate on whether Scotland should have its own channel (outside BBC Alba, the Gaelic language broadcaster). Research that the BBC Trust commissioned in 2007 showed that the changes brought about by devolution were not taken into consideration in the central London-based BBC news programming, which was still produced to a great extent from an Anglo-centric perspective (BBC Trust, 2008). In its first administration at the Scottish parliament, the SNP appointed the Scottish Broadcasting Commission to look into the broadcasting landscape in Scotland. Their recommendation was to introduce a separate Scottish public service broadcaster to serve the nation exclusively, but this was not acted upon at the time, as broadcasting was reserved to Westminster and the SNP had to focus its attention on the independence referendum after its 2011 victory. However, a few years after the 2014 referendum, the BBC announced its own initiative of a £30 million investment in a new channel to fund the production of both news and entertainment content for a Scottish audience.

The 2014 referendum, however, was widely seen as an occasion where the power of traditional media, like television and newspapers, was challenged. Grassroots groups reinvigorated the debate on social media and contested the dominance of traditional news platforms (Law, 2015). Traditional media are generally seen less as the exclusive carriers of political debate in a digital age, particularly in regard to their ability to reach younger audiences. During the referendum a range of dedicated websites emerged to debate the case for and against independence, though many of them 'were individual rather than collective, or they spoke to the converted' pro- and anti-independence voters (Hassan, 2014: 85). Debate on social media was significant in volume, but also to a great extent it was restricted among partisan groups whose members held similar positions.

As broader and more widely accessible platforms (considering that in 2014 broadband and PC access remained low in some parts of Scotland, including parts of Glasgow and the west), the press and broadcasting remained important 'in setting the parameters of official political discourse as well as registering the ways in which social media replicate the established patterns of political discourse' (Law, 2015: 7). Traditional media remained influential on political debate in the digital age, and for this reason it is worth studying how they worked in framing the referendum.

Before addressing this question in chapter 4, the next chapter will discuss how news sources, and particularly the two sides of the referendum argument, decided to frame what the referendum decision was about. The present chapter has established the significance of pragmatic considerations as a key factor in Scottish attitudes on the British union throughout its history and the next chapter will argue that, in tune with this, such considerations were also central in the frames promoted by the Yes and No sides in their communication with the media during the campaign.

3

Sources and their frames

As discussed in the previous chapter the two formal campaigns designated to represent the official Yes and No sides were launched in 2012.
This chapter will explore how these two major players framed the referendum campaign based on interviews with the professional communicators who were responsible for media relations on each side. It will also
discuss the role of non-partisan civil society[1] organisations in the framing of the campaign, considering the historical centrality of Scottish civil
society in previous key moments in the constitutional debate.

The Electoral Commission, the independent body responsible for
regulating elections and referendums in the UK, registered a total of
forty-two campaigners in the Scottish referendum, with twenty-one supporting a 'Yes' outcome and twenty-one in support of a 'No' outcome
(Electoral Commission, 2014). Together they spent £6.6 million in campaigning, of which £3.5 million was spent for the No and £3.1 million
for the Yes side (Electoral Commission, 2014). Yes Scotland and Better
Together became the designated lead campaigners for each referendum
outcome following an assessment process of applications undertaken by
the Commission in 2014. The two organisations also invested the highest total spent in campaigning during the referendum: Better Together
spent £1,422,602 and Yes Scotland £1,420,800.

Better Together campaigned for Scotland to stay in the UK and was
made up of the three biggest UK parties with branches in Scotland: Labour,
the Conservatives and the Liberal Democrats. All three had been in government in Westminster or in Scotland in the past – Labour and the
Conservatives on their own, and the Liberal Democrats as part of coalitions. Although the three parties agreed on their stance against Scottish
independence, there were considerable underlying political differences
between them, because they represented different positions in the political spectrum and were essentially political opponents contesting for
government in London and Scotland. There was, therefore, a perceived

need among journalists and the parties themselves to have balance between their individual perspectives.

Each party took part in Better Together campaign activities and at the same time sought to reach their own voters through separate communication tactics. According to one of the parties' communications managers interviewed for this research:

> there had to be a distinctive [party] case ... the job that we really had was to try to identify the [party] vote, identify bits of our vote that were soft and might vote Yes, and try to directly communicate with them, partly by the traditional methods of canvassing, of writing to them, direct mail and that sort of thing.

Yes Scotland was also a coalition of several partners, and included the SNP, the Scottish Green Party and the Scottish Socialist Party. However in this case the SNP was clearly the biggest party in that campaign and the only one that had ever been in government. As discussed in the previous chapter, the SNP had gradually become the most popular party in Scotland in the post-devolution period and was in government at the Scottish parliament at the time of the referendum. Its leader at the time, Scottish First Minister Alex Salmond, was a key figure in the Yes campaign. Neither the Green nor the Socialist parties commanded comparable support, power or prominence in political life at any stage in their history. Although the two smaller parties of Yes Scotland were to an extent visible in the official campaign the balance and relationship between them and the SNP was very different from that within the Better Together camp, because the three parties of the Yes campaign had not been in direct competition with each other. Although, like the Better Together parties, each also engaged in their own communication strategy to persuade their voters, there was less perceived conflict in their positions and the SNP, as the bigger party, was inevitably the most prominent in the campaign, especially as it was also the party that had initiated the referendum and was in government when it took place.

Framing the messages

Both campaigns invested significant resources in communications. In both cases the communications teams were led by non-politicians. Better Together's campaign director was Blair McDougall, a Labour activist who had been an adviser to senior Labour politicians, and the campaign's director of communications for most of its duration was Rob Shorthouse, who had previously worked as communications adviser for the Scottish government and Strathclyde Police. Yes Scotland's chief executive was Blair Jenkins, former head of News and Current Affairs at STV and BBC Scotland. Both communications teams eventually encompassed the heads of communications of each of the participating parties, who in the last few months before the referendum worked from the central campaign offices. Overall, in the last few months, the communications teams on each side comprised between six and eight people. These communication teams were in regular contact with the media, providing information, placing interviews, organising events for the media to cover, arranging for their representatives to appear in interviews and broadcast debates, and alerting channels to public appearances of their leading figures.

In addition to the media campaign, the strategy of the Yes side was to involve ordinary citizens and local communities from the early stages, so that the Yes campaign would become a 'movement' rather than a top-down political campaign. Their strategy involved asking those who supported independence to persuade others in their communities, their workplace and social circle, and to mobilise support at grassroots level through local groups and public meetings. According to a communicator from the Yes campaign interviewed for this research:

> most of the work we did from the beginning was to do with setting up local Yes groups around the country, and trying to make sure we had the structure there to get as many people involved as possible. Which started with the people who were already in favour of independence, but with the intention that they would build and grow as quickly as possible.

As discussed in the previous chapter, in 2012 when the campaign was launched, support for independence in opinion polls was under 30 per cent. The same communicator suggested that the Yes campaign's strategy to overturn that figure was based on using existing supporters to spread messages in their immediate environment:

> if everyone who is going to vote Yes already can persuade one other person, then we have a majority. So I started saying at that time, your job, if you want Yes, your job is to promote it to people you know, persuade one other person. And that conversational model became very important.

The Yes side therefore encouraged and nurtured a significant grassroots movement which was active in traditional campaigning, namely canvassing, local groups and local public meetings, but also on digital media through dedicated pro-independence websites. According to another political communicator interviewed for this project, 'a huge part of the Yes campaign was based on engaging people in their own communities, through community work, through canvassing door to door, through local events, local initiatives, local public meetings'. Dedicated pro-independence grassroots groups formed during the campaign (for example, Women for Independence, Working for Scotland) and with their parallel communication activities they tried to mobilise the public and ignite debate. In fact, this public mobilisation strategy was so central in the campaign that the Yes communicators interviewed for this project felt strongly that Yes Scotland was not a traditional campaign but a movement, and this was at the centre of how they presented their messages to the media.

The rationale behind this approach was that, according to Yes communication strategists, people are more likely to be persuaded by people they know, rather than by mainstream media or politicians, who, according to them, had lost public trust. According to one of the interviewees:

> people are more influenced by people they know and like in their own community than they are by people on television or politicians. ... We thought our best chance of winning was to not be part of the normal political circus, but to be something different. To look and feel and sound like something different, a people's campaign, and genuinely do that, build a grassroots movement, which is what we did.

The same interviewee said that this was also their way of dealing with what they expected would be a hostile press; as explained in the previous chapter most newspapers were either against or sceptical about independence. Anticipating unfavourable coverage through the mainstream press, the campaign sought alternative, non-mediated routes to communicate its messages.

At the same time, part of Yes Scotland's media relations strategy was to have non-politicians speaking for the campaign in the media as often as possible. Of course the key figures appearing in the media for Yes were still high-profile politicians, such as Alex Salmond, then leader of the SNP and First Minister of Scotland, Nicola Sturgeon, then deputy SNP leader, and Patrick Harvey, then leader of the Scottish Green Party. Alongside them, though, communications strategists of the Yes campaign endeavoured:

> as often as we could in newspaper articles, or television, or radio, or in public meetings, as much as we possibly could we would always prefer to use people who were not politicians. ... We knew that for Yes to succeed it had to be seen as being bigger than party politics and it had to be seen as about the future of the country, not as a party political debate.

The No campaign, on the other hand, originally functioned as a more traditional political campaign, led by senior political figures like Alistair Darling, former Labour Chancellor of the Exchequer and chairman of

Better Together, or former UK prime minister Gordon Brown, whose profile in Scotland remained high during and after his administration, and whose interventions towards the end of the campaign were perceived as particularly significant in the No camp. As mentioned earlier each party in Better Together also ran their own campaigns aiming to persuade their own voters and this is something the party communicators from Better Together interviewed for this research were quite emphatic about. According to one of them, 'we wanted to speak to our people, but we also wanted to speak together, as a cross-party campaign, so we did both'.

Although the interviewees from the No side of the argument did not suggest any tension between the party communication strategies and the umbrella campaign, it was clear that having a separate party communication plan and messages to address their specific party voters was important for them. On the other hand, they did not mention grassroots campaigning as part of their strategy, and indeed, although volunteers for both sides were involved in canvassing, the communication strategy of Better Together was primarily based on more traditional methods, such as identifying and targeting undecided voters through databases and persuading voters of the parties to follow the party line.

Having provided a general overview of the two campaigns' overall communication strategy, I will now discuss the frames that each campaign promoted in their media relations. As seen in chapter 1, frames are here understood as definitions of what the referendum decision was about, as revealed through interviews with political communicators who worked with the media on either side of the argument. In these interviews respondents from the official campaigns, or the political parties that made them up, were asked what their key messages to the media were and what the referendum was about for them. Their responses were organised into seven frames, discussed below with corresponding evidence from the interviews. After presenting these frames, I will examine the extent to which there is any evidence that they were shared or endorsed by the public. Finally I will discuss political communicators' and civil society actors' views on the *strategic game* frame, which was found rather prominently in the media coverage (as will be seen in chapter 4) even though it was not actively promoted by the communicators themselves.

The *self-determination* and *social justice* frames

The key messages of each campaign, as outlined by the communicators interviewed, provide an insight into how each side decided to frame what the referendum decision was about. For Yes Scotland, their central slogan, 'Scotland's future in Scotland's hands', reflects a framing of the referendum as being about democratic self-determination, hereafter referred to as the *self-determination* frame. As an interviewee from the Yes side put it:

> the central proposition ... was that the best people to make decisions about what's right for Scotland are the people of Scotland. The people who live here, who work here.

As seen in the previous chapter, the idea that Scotland did not have enough self-determination within the UK gained ground mostly in the post-war period of the twentieth century and peaked during the Thatcher years, when the perception that Scotland's interests were not catered for by the UK government intensified. This eventually led to devolution in the late 1990s. As explained previously, a sense of democratic deficit and dissatisfaction with how Scottish affairs were managed by Westminster was central in Scotland's history in the union and formed the basis of tension several times. Another interviewee from the Yes side reflected the same frame of *self-determination* by evoking narratives that have deep historical roots:

> a Yes vote would have, if you like, would have unlocked the door to the better democratic position being brought into place, where people in Scotland can vote for future political party manifestos and, if enough people vote for such a thing, that's what happens. ... For many people it was a vote to assert that democratic principle, that how people in Scotland vote should determine how we are governed, as opposed to at the moment, for example, where we've got a Conservative government at Westminster, which obviously governs in Scotland, but the Conservative party have only got one single MP in the whole of Scotland.

The decline of the Conservative Party in Scotland over the second half of the twentieth century culminated in the 1980s and 1990s, as was discussed in the previous chapter. It was in that period that narratives of a democratic deficit emerged more prominently, according to which Scotland was ruled by a Westminster government it did not elect, given that Scotland at that time elected primarily Labour MPs. These narratives are echoed in the perspective of the interviewee above. Although, following devolution, the Scottish Conservatives achieved some representation in the Scottish parliament they consistently lagged behind both Labour and the Liberal Democrats, at least until 2014. At Westminster, Scottish Conservative MPs were even fewer: in the 2010 and 2015 general elections there was only one Conservative MP elected in a Scottish seat.

Indeed, Labour too was soon to find itself in a similar position, with only one Scottish MP in the 2015 Westminster election. As noted in the previous chapter, the big Westminster parties gradually lost much of their legitimacy in Scotland, further reinforcing a sense of democratic deficit, which is what the interviewee reflects on here.

The *self-determination* frame represents the 2014 referendum as a decision on democratic self-determination, on Scotland running its own affairs, determining its own future, making its own decisions and/or getting the governments it votes for. The *self-determination* frame does not necessarily make reference to specific decisions that would be made differently if Scotland became independent, but it is about the bigger issue of addressing this perceived democratic deficit that, according to this frame, Scotland has experienced and will continue to experience inside the United Kingdom. The frame promotes self-determination primarily as a democratic principle, as the interviewee above suggests.

Another frame also promoted by Yes Scotland, alongside *self-determination*, saw the referendum as a decision on making Scotland a fairer society. This frame is referred to hereafter as the *social justice* frame. According to an interviewee from the Yes side, one of their key messages was that 'an independent Scotland would be a fairer country, would have a greater commitment to social justice'. By social justice the Yes campaign meant closing the gap between the more and less affluent groups in society and sharing resources more equally among different social groups. This was also supported by another interviewee from the same side who suggested that the referendum 'was about the ability – by deciding and choosing a different economic policy in Scotland – to have a fairer distribution of wealth, on the basis of the UK being one of the most unequal countries in the developed world'. The argument of the Yes campaign was that an independent Scotland would make policy decisions that would enable what in their view would be a fairer distribution of wealth, however the specific policy decisions were not mentioned as part of this frame. Although notionally it is connected to the *policy* frame, the *social justice* frame is more abstract and more value-oriented, while the *policy* frame is pragmatic and makes specific references to individual policies.

The *policy* frame

Self-determination and *social justice* were conceived broadly as abstract values, whereas the proposition that the referendum was a decision about policy, hereafter referred to as the *policy frame*, connected the referendum vote to its impact on a range of specific policy areas, including the economy, welfare, military security, health and education, or even childcare and broadcasting. This was a frame promoted by both the Yes and the No campaigns. For the SNP, which was also the party in government, the referendum was a decision about the proposals outlined in the Scottish government's White Paper for Independence, which was published in November 2013. As a member of the party's communications team explained:

> the White Paper ... defined the exact prospectus of what an independent Scotland would be like. And of course in a referendum, people need to be very clear what they are voting for, or indeed what they are voting against. And in a formal sense, people were voting for or against independence as defined in the Scottish government's White Paper.

The framing of political events, such as elections or referendums, as a decision on policy issues is well-documented in analyses of mediated political communication, as was seen in chapter 1. Often contrasted with the *game* frame, which focuses on political style and process, the *issue* or *policy* frame involves an understanding of voting as choosing between different political actors' policy proposals (Lawrence, 2000). As discussed in chapter 1, it can be identified in texts that contain references to policy issues, the proposals of politicians about them and their impact for the public (Lawrence, 2000). Lawrence (2000) suggests that it is more common in the media during the early stages of a political debate, while when a decision actually needs to be made, it is superseded by a focus on the competition of the campaign.

The Scottish government's White Paper contained considerable detail on how a variety of policy areas would be managed in an independent Scotland. These included economic policy and broader governance, such as the management of healthcare, defence, welfare, or the role of the monarchy. Most interviewees – from the campaigns, the media and civil society – attributed the presence of the *policy* frame in the debate to this particular focus in the Yes side's communication strategy. This could be because the White Paper was a concrete official document whose launch was a central event in the referendum campaign; however, the Yes side was certainly not the only actor promoting the *policy* frame.

The parties in Better Together also saw the referendum as a decision about policy, primarily about economic policy consequences and the perceived risks that independence would pose to what, in their view, were the benefits Scotland enjoyed as part of the United Kingdom. According to a communications director at one of the Better Together parties, their key message was 'the economic cost to Scotland, the cost in terms of jobs, the economic black hole in the Nationalists' plans'.

Interviewees from the No side said that their decision to focus on economic policy was based on polling which showed that this was the area that would sway how people were prepared to vote, particularly in relation to the perceived risk of losing economic security. This is in line with previous research, which suggests that economic consequences are key in major political decisions (de Vreese *et al.*, 2001).

Indeed many of the polls that Better Together commissioned in the months leading up to the referendum, which are available in the public domain (http://whatscotlandthinks.org/search?query=&clients=Better+ Together), explore Scots' attitudes on different policy issues, from the economy to pensions and healthcare. This also confirms interviewees' suggestion that Better Together was equally focused on framing the campaign in policy terms.

Moreover, it has been shown that messages which emphasise possible losses resulting from a political decision are more persuasive than messages that provide information on potential benefits (Heilman and Miclea, 2016). In other national referendums in different contexts, negative messages about risk are thought to have been so emotionally compelling that they are believed to have reversed trends established in public opinion polls and given the victory to the side that promoted them (Atickan, 2015). In this specific case, the focus on what would be lost from losing membership of the British union was thus seen as a potentially powerful message that could supersede arguments on the benefits of independence.

Whether used by the Yes side, to highlight the new policies that would come into effect in an independent Scotland, or by the No side, to emphasise the risks to existing policies if Scotland was to lose the 'safety' of the union, the *policy* frame presented the referendum as being about its practical implications. It suggested that the decision should be made based on whether voters believed policies affecting their lives would be better under independence or under the union. In other words it was a 'pragmatic' frame (Castelló and Capdevila, 2013).

Apart from the potential of policy to sway voters, the political communicators interviewed believed that this frame had better chance to attract people to engage in the referendum debate. The question that was on the ballot paper was a strictly constitutional one, but a debate on an exclusively constitutional issue was seen as potentially dull. According to a member of the Yes campaign communications team:

We knew that if the debate was a dry constitutional debate, if it was just about flags and borders and constitutions, it wouldn't get people excited. So we knew we had to translate independence into things that people care about in their daily lives. So we were very much encouraging people to think about what impact it would have on public services, what impact it would have on job security, on things like the role of carers in society, the NHS became a big issue.

An interviewee from a civil society organisation agreed that a purely constitutional debate would have been boring:

> It's no surprise that the media picked it up and run with it as a sort of way to cover the debate, because policy is also a bit more interesting than the constitutional framework. Can you imagine trying to cover an argument about constitutional framework for two years? There's less to talk about.

Perhaps though, the two reasons examined so far behind the Yes and No campaigns' decision to frame the referendum as a question on policy, namely its potential persuasiveness and its capacity to make the debate more interesting and engaging, were not the only reasons it was chosen by the two sides. As was discussed in detail in the previous chapter, Scotland's position in the British union had long been defined in policy terms. Scotland's identity itself has also been defined as 'a more explicitly political identity' (Johns and Mitchell, 2016: 54) or a different 'prism for translating social change into political meaning and action' (McCrone, 2005b: 79) rather than a traditional ethnic identity. Even if cultural, symbolic notions of national identity remain strong in how Scots define themselves, as seen in the previous chapter, a civic understanding of Scottishness had long dominated official public discourse and is in line with a framing of the referendum debate as a pragmatic, policy related decision.

Therefore, the choice to frame the referendum as a decision on specific policies additionally resonated with the longer history of the official political discourse regarding the relationship between Scotland and the union. Arguably the union originally came together due to the benefits it promised for Scotland's economic future and military security (Devine, 2016); previous challenges to the union were based on pragmatic arguments suggesting that Scotland was treated unfairly in policy terms (Paterson, 2015); and these were in turn refuted with arguments that leaving the union would result in major disruption to the perceived benefits in different policy areas that Scotland enjoyed within the United Kingdom.

The decision made by campaign strategists on both sides to use a frame that had been so long part of Scotland's public debates around its position in Britain arguably also helped the campaigns make the most of voters' awareness of arguments from the past. This was the first time Scots were called to vote on independence but the Scottish autonomy debate was not a new issue at all, as explained in chapter 2. Choosing a frame with historical roots allowed both campaigns to tap into voters' memories and previous associations with the issue, which were not as much about symbolic understandings of identity as about more tangible disagreements on governance.

Although each side used the *policy* frame differently, to highlight contrasting arguments in favour and against independence, the frame was claimed by both campaigns. This was not just a case of 'campaign dialogue' (Hanggli and Kriesi, 2012), whereby one side 'owns' the frame and the other side responds to their arguments by using the same frame (although some degree of such dialogue did take place with each side forced to respond to the arguments put forward by their opponents). In this case, however, as suggested by the interview excerpts above, both sides decided that the *policy* frame was a strategically beneficial way for them to promote their preferred outcome and they used it 'offensively' (Hanggli and Kriesi, 2010) to propose original arguments supporting their side, as well as 'defensively' to counter the arguments proposed by their opponents.

It is indeed possible for the same frame to include a range of pro-, anti- and neutral arguments and to be used by opposing sides in a debate (Nisbet, 2010). Like other generic frames, the *policy* frame has no 'inherent valance' (de Vreese, 2004: 40). Each campaign had 'ownership' over specific agenda items (for example the issue of whether or not an independent Scotland would maintain the British pound as its currency was promoted by Better Together; while the issue of a potential increase of the private sector's role in the NHS if Scotland remained in the union was promoted by Yes Scotland). However neither campaign had ownership of the overall frame that represented the debate as being about policy decisions.

In addition to this, the officially neutral civil society representatives interviewed also suggested that their messages during the campaign were about *policy*. Depending on the groups they represented they said that they communicated about issues directly affecting their members, like funding or jurisdiction, or about broader issues such as the degree of voters' engagement with the referendum; but also about policy areas such as poverty, welfare or nuclear disarmament. According to one civil society interviewee:

> [our organization] has for over thirty years been against nuclear weapons and in favour of unilateral disarmament so regardless of the yes or no, that's a key issue for us. So that was something that we didn't shirk away from during that time.

Although the specific agenda of policy issues that civil society representatives wanted to see discussed during the referendum campaign might
have sometimes been different from that of the political sides, the
former did not contest the assumption that the referendum was about
policy. Still, all civil society interviewees agreed that it was not them who
framed the media debate as being about *policy*. They all felt that their
role in the coverage was only a small supplement to the main debate that
was happening primarily between political elites, where neutral sources
had a marginal role. As one of them put it:

> So we're not pretending that we knocked, you know, the straightforward
> Yes–No stories off the telly. We kind of sat below that and because we were
> quite interesting, and because at times the debate got so dull, we were used
> in that way [to bring in a different point of view]. I mean we knew we were
> being used in that way and we were quite happy for that.

Thus the role of civil society organisations in 2014 was considerably less
important compared to previous key moments examined in chapter 1,
including the 1997 devolution referendum. According to Paterson and
Wyn Jones (1999: 193), Scottish civil society had traditionally enjoyed
'a long record of leading popular opinion' and its support of devolution
in the 1980s and 1990s 'lent its credibility to the entire project of home
rule'. By contrast, in 2014 civil society had a more marginal presence in
the debate, possibly due to the neutral stance many of these organisations officially adopted. As will be seen in the next chapter, this view
that neutral sources had a minor role in the framing of the referendum is
supported by evidence regarding both the prominence of different news
sources in the coverage and interviews with journalists on the factors
that influenced media frames.

The *national identity* frame

In a referendum on national independence one might expect *national
identity* to play a significant role in campaign discourse, perhaps even
more so than *policy*. However, as already explained in chapter 2, in
modern politics ethnic definitions of identity tend to be avoided by
mainstream politicians, as they can be seen as discriminatory and can
fail to resonate with an increasingly ethnically diverse electorate. As discussed in the previous chapter, Scottish nationalism consistently adopted
a civic form from the 1980s onwards, focusing on the shared values that
were perceived to make Scots distinctive rather than their ethnic origins
(Johns and Mitchell, 2016). A manifestation of this civic-minded definition of Scottishness by political elites is that in both the 1997 and the

2014 referendums, the franchise included all Scottish residents even if they had been born outside Scotland, while Scottish born voters who lived outside the region did not have the right to participate.

Perhaps for some of these reasons, the idea that the referendum was about national identity was not promoted by either official campaign. For the Yes campaign it would have been risky to ascribe to an ethnic form of nationalism, when Scottish society was increasingly diverse; and for the No side it might have been challenging to promote a notion of unified British identity in a nation where the electorate identified primarily as Scottish, as seen in the previous chapter.

The political communicators interviewed from the Yes side argued that for their campaign the referendum was about *self-determination*, *social justice* and *policy*. The No side used primarily pragmatic *policy* frames as well, and also proposed that the referendum was about Scotland maintaining the benefits of being part of the UK while increasing its autonomy in the devolution settlement, a proposition which will be discussed subsequently under the *constitutional change* frame.

Interviewees who supported a No outcome, however, sometimes accused the Yes side of using an *identity* frame in their campaign. For example one of the political communicators interviewed argued that, 'what the Nationalists wanted to do was basically to frame the question as "are you Scottish or not?" and quite a lot of people did assert their Scottishness by voting Yes'. Another interviewee suggested that 'it was portrayed as, if you were confident about being Scottish, you obviously went for a Scottish independent parliament, and if you weren't that confident, or you were scared, then you voted to stay with what you had'.

There is no evidence in this study that such a framing of the referendum decision was part of the Yes Scotland discourse: neither the interviews with Yes communicators nor the analysis of the coverage showed the Yes side making any such claims. In fact, one of the interviewees from the Yes campaign argued that promoting a *national identity* frame would not have appealed to a large part of the electorate and thus they chose a pragmatic approach instead:

> there would always be a section of the Scottish population who would support independence just because they think Scotland is its own country and we should be independent and more like a classic European nationalism, if you like, where we should be independent just because we're different … But that was never going to be the majority of people in Scotland.

As I will discuss in the next chapter, the *identity* frame, which describes the referendum as being a decision about national identity and involves references to Scottish distinctiveness, or references to the features and history that Scots share with the rest of the UK, was generally not prominent in media discourse either.

The constitutional change frame

The proposition that the referendum was not just about independence but about a change in the constitutional status of Scotland within the British union, hereafter referred to as the *constitutional change* frame, suggests that the referendum was an opportunity for the Scottish parliament to gain more powers in addition to the ones it already had. According to one interviewee from a television channel:

> I suppose that's really what the referendum was about: more powers. But the referendum really was about how to deliver more powers: is it within a Westminster context or an independent Scotland?

This frame involved an emphasis on achieving more powers for Scotland or changing the constitutional status of Scotland; and reports on proposals for a federal UK, or 'devo-max' (a term commonly used to describe enhanced devolution). Although it was the most popular option according to opinion polls, increased devolution for Scotland did not officially appear on the ballot paper. Eventually, though, all parties of the Better Together campaign committed to deliver more powers to the Scottish parliament if the outcome was against independence. Initially they did this separately through the length of the campaign and in the final week in the form of a commitment signed by their three leaders on the front page of the *Daily Record*. As explained in the previous chapter, 'the Vow' effectively was seen as replacing the status quo option on the ballot paper, and putting increased devolution on the table as an option (Johns and Mitchell, 2016; Mullen, 2016). Although the context was different, this campaign strategy is reminiscent of that adopted by the No campaign in the 1980 Quebec independence referendum where a No vote was equated with 'renewed federalism' (Pammett and LeDuc, 2001).

Therefore, especially in the final weeks of the campaign, the *constitutional change* frame was promoted by the No side. As one interviewee from the No side suggested:

> the big key message was the best of both worlds. That's what people wanted, they wanted to know that there was going to be a strong Scottish parliament and a future for a strong country, but they also wanted the security of the United Kingdom behind them.

As the referendum campaign progressed it appeared increasingly that this 'best of both worlds' would need to involve some expansion of the powers of the Scottish parliament. Arguably this may have been a position that the No side was forced to adopt in response to polls showing increasing numbers of voters were prepared to vote for independence (YouGov, 2014). As mentioned previously, surveys had long showed that enhanced devolution was the option most voters would prefer (Mitchell, 2016a: 81; Mullen, 2016: 17) and identifying a vote for No with a vote for increased devolution was an attempt to influence voters towards the end of the campaign.

At the same time, this move brought into focus the *constitutional change* frame that presented the referendum as a choice on how Scotland could best secure the optimum degree of autonomy, inside or outside the union. As I argue elsewhere (Dekavalla, 2016), the editorials of all Scottish indigenous newspapers in the final week of the campaign framed the referendum as a decision on how more powers or 'change' for Scotland might be best achieved – within the union with increased jurisdiction for the Scottish parliament or outside the union as an independent country. As will be seen in the next chapter, the *constitutional change* frame was only particularly prominent at the end of the campaign, but it managed to a great extent to frame the important final part of the decision-making.

The *divorce* frame

The *divorce* frame, which represented the referendum as the potential dissolution of a marriage or relationship, was expressed through relationship and breaking up metaphors which represented Scotland and England as human partners or friends falling out. This frame was also adaptable by both sides: in some cases the divorce was difficult and undesirable, while in others it was the resolution of a problematic relationship.

The frame was not mentioned by interviewees from either the Yes or No campaigns as an understanding of the referendum that they actively promoted. Only one political communicator from the No side referred to it, but he made it clear that this was his personal perception of what the referendum was about, which he felt did not resonate with the way voters saw it:

> For me it was about the future of the country that I am from, Great Britain, and the issue for me was, are we going to keep this country together, or are we going to divide it? … People weren't swayed by emotional messages about Britain, or, you know, about sticking together as one big happy family … They were very pragmatic and I'm pretty sure both sides would agree with that.

Although this interviewee suggests that the frame was not particularly central in the No campaign, and implies that its appeal with voters was limited, the *divorce* frame was used quite heavily in David Cameron's 'No going back' speech, delivered in Aberdeen three days before the vote on 15 September 2014:

> This is a decision that could break up our family of nations, and rip Scotland from the rest of the UK. And we must be very clear. There's no going back from this. No re-run. This is a once-and-for-all decision. If Scotland votes yes, the UK will split, and we will go our separate ways forever. (Cameron cited in the *Independent*, 2014)

The excerpt above contains several family metaphors ('break up', 'family of nations', 'split', 'go our separate ways') and is one of the most representative examples of the *divorce* frame in the news coverage. This suggests that the frame was used in official campaign discourse, even if it did not frame their main messages. Perhaps on this occasion it was used as a further attempt to construct emotionally compelling frames that have been considered effective in changing voters' opinions in different referendum contexts (Atickan, 2015).

Faith in London institutions
All the frames discussed so far in this chapter were also identified in the media coverage, as I will explain in the next chapter. Only one frame emerged from the interviews, which was not found in the media coverage: that the referendum decision was about faith in political institutions. According to this frame, which was proposed by two interviewees, one from the No side and one from a civil society organisation, the referendum was an opportunity to express people's disappointment and low trust in Westminster politics, particularly after recent perceived failures like the 2008 politicians' expenses scandal, the handling of the economic crisis, the protection of bankers' financial status. According to one of the political communicators interviewed:

> in an era when politicians and institutions ... faith in them has never been as low, I think, in my lifetime, there was a massive protest vote, which I think is ongoing. ... Our politicians, our banks, when you have a global kind of downturn like this, it does appear like politicians can do nothing about it and the institution of Westminster itself, after the expenses ... I don't think it has recovered from the expenses scandal, so I think a number of people voted against that.

This frame was not promoted by either campaign, which might explain its absence from the media coverage. As will be seen in subsequent chapters, frames that were promoted by the official campaigns had more presence in the coverage of the referendum. Yet mistrust in the London government had historically been a key issue in Scotland's relationship with the union, even during the very early years (Devine, 2016). More recently, mistrust in London institutions was also behind Labour's loss of popularity in Scotland in the 2000s, as discussed in the previous chapter. It could therefore be that a tension between centre and periphery underlied much of the debate without being explicitly expressed as a distinctive media frame. According to an interviewee from a civil society organisation:

> A lot of people would argue that they were voting Yes because they don't trust Westminster and they don't trust MPs and they wanted to get rid of the old system, so it was about getting rid of the establishment and trying to create something new. But I don't think that really came out in the sort of media conversation because that might be … because the media is establishment too, so why would they want you to see that?

LeDuc (2002) suggests that people's attitudes towards individual politicians or the popularity of the sitting government can be important influencing factors in referendum campaigns. When people are generally unhappy with politicians, he suggests, they are likely to vote against what politicians propose, when they all propose the same option. Referendums are even sometimes referred to as second-order elections, which means that their outcome may not only be influenced by the subject that voters are deciding on, but also by how they feel about those in power in the national political arena, the record of the current government, or issues and events which are not directly related to the referendum itself (Heath and Taylor, 1999; LeDuc, 2015).

Clearly the 2014 Scottish referendum was not a second-order election: it generated a level of engagement that no election ever had in Scotland and, at decision time, voters were fully aware of the historical significance of their vote. Still, on one hand, second-order effects are very difficult to avoid altogether in any referendum (LeDuc, 2015: 141), and, on the other, people's perceptions of Westminster politics are an essential part of the issue of Scottish autonomy. How voters assessed the performance of sitting and recent governments at Westminster and Holyrood could understandably impact their views on whether the jurisdiction of either of these parliaments should continue or be extended. Perhaps more than ordinary second-order effects, the issue of national independence is by definition closely connected to how voters viewed specific Scottish and UK administrations.

Still, this frame was not used in official campaign communications, perhaps because Yes Scotland chose the more positive *self-determination* frame, where, as explained earlier, the emphasis was not on how Westminster governments may have 'failed' Scotland, but instead on how an independent Scotland would make its own decisions, separately from England and the rest of the United Kingdom. The *self-determination* frame did not explicitly include any elements proposing lack of faith in Westminster as a causal explanation.

Audience frames?

Many of the interviewees for this project, particularly respondents from civil society and journalists, referred to the different frames above as originating in how the public understood the referendum, rather than in how the official campaigns defined it. A separate research project would be required to establish the extent to which the public also thought of the referendum in these terms and, if they did, the degree to which this was based on their own interpretations or was the result of their exposure to media and campaign messages. Such an enquiry falls outside the scope of this book.

Indirect evidence relating to this question, derived from social media research and opinion polls, suggests that the *policy* frame figured rather prominently in audiences' understanding of the referendum. For example, research on Twitter during the campaign revealed that online debates also focused on policy issues, and particularly economic policy (Fang *et al.*, 2015; Quinlan *et al.*, 2015) and to a lesser extent public services (Quinlan *et al.*, 2015) or nuclear defence (Fang *et al.*, 2015).

Opinion polls carried out regularly in the months ahead of the vote also found that voters rated these and other policy issues as significant in deciding how to vote (TNS-BMRB, 2014), with economic policy appearing as the top issue. However the questionnaires used for these polls themselves set out a list of policy areas and asked respondents to rate them in relation to each other, thus taking as granted that the referendum decision was one about *policy* issues. In these polls the public did not spontaneously mention *policy* issues as key in their understanding of what the referendum decision was about, but respondents were prompted by the poll question itself to choose between various policy issues. Polls therefore provide no evidence that the *policy* frame originated in public opinion, although it was a prominent understanding of the referendum in the public sphere. No poll asked respondents to compare *policy* with other frames, such as *identity* or *self-determination*, in their salience or importance during the referendum.

As will be shown in the next chapter, the *policy* frame was dominant in media debates throughout the campaign, and by the end it was one of the most prominent ways of understanding what was at stake in the vote. Chapter 5 will discuss journalistic factors that may have contributed to making it so prominent in the media and will argue that media framing was influenced by the campaign framing discussed in the present chapter.

This chapter argued that the *policy* frame originated in the Yes and No strategy camps, but at the same time it was chosen by political communicators because of its potential to change voting intentions and to engage voters by making the referendum debate more interesting for them. In other words, it was chosen with the electorate in mind, for the strategic purpose of getting more votes. In this sense the campaigns' framing was influenced by what they thought the public wanted to hear.

At the same time, the *policy* frame generally made sense in the context of the referendum because the Scottish constitutional issue has historically been closely associated with issues of *policy* as argued in this and the previous chapter. It is therefore very difficult to judge conclusively from the evidence available to what extent audience frames were influenced by the 2014 campaign and its media coverage alone. As was argued in the discussion of framing effects in chapter 1, what audiences make of frames depends on their previous political knowledge and experiences as well as the range of different frames they get exposed to from media and non-media sources. What is clear in any case is that campaign and media frames had an impact on which frames were available in the public sphere – the fact that the *policy* frame appeared on social media debates and opinion poll questions lends support to this interpretation.

Apart from *policy*, the other frames discussed above have not been tested in opinion polls or social media research, so it is not possible to establish how they compared in prominence in audiences' considerations. However, existing research on social media debates during the 2014 referendum points to one more frame dominating how audiences talked about the decision: partisan politics and the performance of the two campaign camps (Shephard, 2014), which occupied up to one-third of the Twitter debate at key moments of the campaign (Quinlan *et al.*, 2015). This aspect will be discussed subsequently under the *game* frame.

The *strategic game* frame

The *strategic game* frame is a well-established concept in literature on the media coverage of politics. It constructs a political event as a competition or strategic game between opponents. It involves a focus on opponent sides winning or losing; war and game metaphors; analyses of candidates' performance, style and perception; and references to opinion polls as a measure of how opponents are doing in the competition (Cappella and Jamieson, 1997). As seen in chapter 1, it was originally developed in the work of Jamieson (1992) and Cappella and Jamieson (1997), as well as in other work around the same time (e.g. Mendelsohn, 1993; Patterson, 1993), and it has since been studied, tested and refined by a range of framing scholars (Lawrence, 2000; Strömbäck and Dimitrova, 2006; Strömback and van Aelst, 2010; Aalberg et al., 2012; Dunaway and Lawrence, 2015, among others).

The *strategic game* frame assigns roles to political actors and expectations about the election or referendum outcome: the political event it frames is presented as being about opponents' tactics to win over voters, and the outcome of the vote can only be victory or defeat. This politician-centric frame is commonly contrasted in the literature with frames that focus instead on policy areas (Aalberg et al., 2012). Lawrence (2000) refers to these as 'issue' frames and they correspond to the *policy* frame in this analysis. Both the *strategic game* frame and issue frames are generic frames found in media coverage of a range of topics, particularly in that of elections and referendums, and they are seen as competing ways of constructing politics, as explained in more detail in chapter 1. The issue (or *policy*) frame is associated with promoting substantive deliberation and informed citizenry (Lawrence, 2000) and the *game* frame is seen as contributing to disengaged and cynical citizens (Cappella and Jamieson, 1997). In LeDuc's terms, the *game* frame is about 'the quest for votes' (2015: 144), which he argues does not promote deliberative democracy. Still others, as explained in chapter 1, suggest that audiences prefer game-framed to issue-focused media coverage of politics, which is less likely to capture their interest (Iyengar et al., 2004).

The *game* frame, as would be expected, was not mentioned by any of the political communicators or the civil society sources interviewed here because they did not actively promote it themselves. The *game* frame is widely seen in the literature as a journalistic frame rather than one introduced by political sources (de Vreese, 2012: 367). By contrast, 'substantive' frames, like the ones presented earlier in this chapter, are seen as introduced in public discourse by journalistic sources, such as political campaigns (Hanggli and Kriesi, 2010: 154). As discussed so far, this was also the case in the Scottish referendum, where the two campaigns promoted a number of 'substantive' frames but did not purposefully emphasise the political *game* of the referendum.

Despite this, as will be shown in chapter 4, the *strategic game* frame was the most dominant frame across television and newspapers, especially in the final stages of the campaign. In this respect, the Scottish referendum was not an exception. Other frame analyses of referendums in completely different national contexts also found this frame to be highly prominent (Robinson, 1998; de Vreese and Semetko, 2002, 2004). Particularly nearer the time of the vote, when a decision has to be made, the *game* frame can be expected to dominate over the issue frame (Lawrence, 2000), especially if the two options are close in polls (Dunaway and Lawrence, 2015).

Chapter 5 will explore how the *game* frame emerged in the news coverage of the Scottish referendum and how it competed in the mediated debate with the other frames presented in this chapter. That chapter will propose a range of factors which had an influence on making some of these frames more prominent than others in the coverage of this event.

The media relations communicators from the two sides interviewed did not openly propose that the referendum was a political competition. That said, they did use game and war metaphors when talking about the referendum, which suggests that they did think of it in that way as well. For example:

> In every single debate I did, the *opponent* for the other side was always a career politician.

> We had a difficulty in that we were massively *outgunned* in terms of almost the entire state machine was working for a Yes vote, which presented challenges.

> But given that the initial expectation, not on our part, but on the part of our *opponents* would have been that … you know, that the Yes vote would be probably in the mid-30s on a good day, maybe 35 per cent on a good day, then pushing it to 45 per cent meant that we did many things right in the campaign. We didn't obviously do everything right cause if we had *we would have won*, but I think overall it was a good, positive, in terms of its tenor, it was a very positive, uplifting campaign.

In all the above examples interviewees from both sides of the argument present their relationship with the other side as one of competition or war through metaphorical expressions such as 'opponent' or 'outgunned', and they emphasise the significance of polls in measuring their success in winning over voters (all of which are indicators of the *game* frame, as explained earlier in this section). Campaign communicators did not suggest that they purposefully communicated these messages to the media, but it seems that they too perceived the referendum as a competition.

In the context of UK elections, it has been found that political sides do in fact promote a focus on the game of the campaign in order to serve their own purposes or to turn voters against their opponents. For example in the 2015 UK general election, parties did not provide opportunities where journalists could question their policy proposals and thus encouraged the media to focus on their staged campaign events instead, while the Conservative Party drove the media's attention toward the possibility of a Labour–SNP post-election coalition in order to gain electoral ground (Cushion *et al.*, 2016). This kind of strategy did not appear to be equally evident in the case of the referendum studied here – both the communication strategists and the broadcasters interviewed (as will be seen in chapter 5) acknowledged that the official campaigns primarily promoted *policy* frames. This does not mean that they had no contribution at all in the prominence of the *game* frame: to mention one example, Yes campaigners did accuse the No side of running a 'negative campaign' in their public appearances, which was an aspect that was further taken up in journalistic questioning.

Moreover, all communicators interviewed suggested that the tactics they used were similar to those used in election campaigns. The main differences they identified between the 2014 referendum and an ordinary election were the intensity of the campaign, the fact that this was a one-off decision that could not be reversed, the fact that there were only two options to choose between, and the fact that voters were a lot more interested in the referendum than in ordinary elections. All this meant that much more was at stake for them and they needed to invest additional effort to reach voters, but in general the media relations strategies and tactics they used were the same as in elections. Some of them had worked on election campaigns before and others came directly from roles in the media industry, but they all had more experience with elections than with referendums. The *strategic game* frame is a well-established frame in the representation of election campaigns and perhaps one part of the reason it is also prominent in referendums is that political actors often treat referendums like elections. Still, there is no concrete evidence from interviews with either group of respondents, that this was a core element of the strategy of either political camp in the 2014 referendum.

This chapter has identified a number of frames from the interviews with key sources that were used by the media during the campaign. The following chapter will explore the extent to which these frames were prominent in the news coverage, particularly on television and in newspapers. As will be shown, all of the frames promoted by political communicators were present in the coverage, albeit to different degrees. Three frames appeared in the media which were not promoted by any sources: the *strategic game* frame, which was one of the most prominent representations of the referendum, and the *national division* and *democratic achievement* frames which received considerably less attention.

Note

1 Civil society is here understood as organisations 'distinct from the state, but including economic society, the various institutions and practices of production and exchange, as well as the institutions and practices of cultural production and reproduction' (Paterson and Wyn Jones, 1999), for example professional associations, unions, voluntary bodies, social movements, churches or the third sector.

4

The media framing of the referendum

This chapter explores the relative prominence of different frames in the news coverage of the campaign through content analysis in two media: television and print newspapers. It first operationalises each of the frames identified, by explaining what elements in the texts were used as indicators, or evidence of the presence of each frame in the analysis. It then discusses the selection of outlets for each medium and the samples analysed. Overall the analysis included sixty-four hours of news and current affairs television coverage produced for a Scottish audience and 3,415 newspaper articles in ten Scottish daily and Sunday newspaper titles. Finally it discusses in detail the relative prominence of frames in different media outlets and shows that two frames dominated the debate across all media. It argues that the balance of frames was very similar across all outlets studied, which suggests a very homogeneous mediated debate.

The frames

Nine frames were identified and analysed in the coverage, most of which were discussed in chapter 3, as they also emerged in the interviews with political communicators from the two campaigns and with civil society representatives. In this section each frame is operationalised by setting out the elements of texts that were used as identifiers of the frame in the content analysis. The first two are generic frames that were also identified in other studies of elections and referendums, as previously discussed. All the other frames were developed specifically for this study, through a thematic analysis of the media content.

The elements that comprise the *strategic game* and *policy* frames were outlined in previous discussion in chapters 1 and 3. Neither frame is unique to the Scottish referendum. As previously explained they were both originally conceptualised in the coverage of political events in other contexts and have been found in news about elections and referendums internationally. To summarise here what was discussed in more detail in previous chapters, evidence of the presence of the *strategic game* frame in a news item consists of: emphasis on the strategy of the Yes and No sides; use of war, game and horserace language; emphasis on who is winning or losing; reports of how the two sides are doing in opinion polls; and analyses of politicians' performance, style and perception – these are the criteria set out by Capella and Jamieson (1997). Evidence of the *policy* frame in the texts includes references to policy issues, the proposals of politicians about them and their impact for the public (Lawrence, 2000). A deductive approach (Semetko and Valkenburg, 2000: 94) was therefore adopted in measuring the strategic game and the issue (or *policy*) frame, which means that the indicators used to identify them were those proposed in the literature on these frames.

Apart from the *game* and *policy* frames, the analysis also identified inductively, operationalised and measured seven other, issue-specific frames, which represented the referendum respectively as a decision regarding *national identity*, democratic *self-determination*, *constitutional change*, *social justice*, a *divorce*, a *democratic achievement*, and a source of *national division*. The first five of these were discussed in the previous chapter since they also emerged in the definitions of the referendum that political and non-political sources provided in interviews. The last two emerged from the news coverage alone. Qualitative thematic analysis was used on the news coverage to identify the problem definition (Entman, 1993) proposed by each frame and the textual elements that manifested each of these seven problem definitions in the media.

Some of these frames were used by both sides of the argument: depending on which side was promoting the frame, a different 'treatment recommendation' (Entman, 1993) was proposed. For instance, when the *national identity* frame was used by the No side, the common identity Scots shared with the rest of the UK meant that the solution to the referendum question was for Scotland to stay in the union. When it was used by the Yes side, the differences that made Scots nationally distinctive necessitated a separation from the UK.

Only the verbal text of the news items was included in this analysis, in order to make the elements of these issue-specific frames comparable with the generic frames presented above. The elements that manifest each frame in the coverage, which resulted from the thematic analysis, were used as indicators to measure the presence of the frames and will be outlined subsequently under each frame.

The *national identity* frame presents the referendum as being a decision about national identity, whether that is British or Scottish. In either case, the decision facing the Scottish electorate would be determined by their sense of belonging to a national community, defined by common values, traditions and a common past. The frame involves references to Scottish distinctiveness, or references to the common features and history that Scots share with the rest of the UK. These were the elements used as indicators in the content analysis. The frame tended to define national identity primarily in civic rather than ethnic terms – as seen in chapter 2 this is a common feature of modern political discourse.

The *self-determination* frame represents the referendum as a choice on whether Scotland should make political decisions separately from the rest of the UK. References to Scotland running its own affairs, determining its own future, making its own decisions or getting the governments it votes for were all indicators of this frame. This frame was promoted by the Yes campaign.

The *constitutional change* frame proposes that the referendum was about a change in the constitutional status of Scotland within the British union, about whether Scotland could secure more governance powers through independence or increased devolution. References to more powers for the Scottish parliament, devolution plus or 'devo-max' (both commonly used terms to describe increased devolution) were the elements indicating this frame in the coverage. This was a frame promoted by Better Together.

The *social justice* frame presents the decision as being about making Scotland a fairer society. Like the *self-determination* frame, the *social justice* frame did not necessarily make reference to the specific ways in which Scotland would become more fair – in many of the cases when it was mentioned in the news coverage by Yes politicians (like *self-determination*, this was also a Yes frame) it was left vague. In the cases where fairness was linked to a more specific claim, this had to do with economic and/or welfare equality, though again no specific policies were mentioned. Therefore the indicators of this frame were references to Scotland becoming a more fair or equal society, or direct references to social justice taking priority in an independent Scotland.

The *divorce* frame represents the referendum as the potential dissolution of a marriage or relationship. It was primarily manifested through family, friendship and relationship metaphors whereby Scotland and England were constructed as human partners or friends falling out. In some cases, when it was used by Better Together sources, the divorce was difficult and undesirable, while in others, when used by the Yes campaign, it was the much-needed but civilised resolution of a difficult relationship.

The *democratic achievement* frame sees the referendum as a major achievement of the Scottish people, due to the high involvement of citizens in grassroots democracy and debate, the high turnout at the polls and the civility with which the referendum was carried out. According to this frame, the outcome of the referendum was not as important as the democratic engagement Scotland had achieved during the campaign. This frame emerged only in the final stage of the referendum and saw it as having a deeper impact on Scottish public life irrespective of whether voters decided to stay or leave the UK. It did not favour either of the political sides and thus it was not among the messages promoted by them. It emerged primarily in media coverage, where it was manifested through references to the unprecedented engagement of voters in the referendum debate, the large participation in public events and in the vote itself, the civilised nature of the independence debate and the lack of violent incidents throughout the campaign. Especially in the last few days of the coverage, this frame was very noticeable across different media.

Another issue-specific frame that was not promoted by political sources and emerged in the media alone was the *national division* frame, according to which the referendum was a cause of division in Scotland, whatever the outcome, because the issue of independence was highly conflictive. Like the *democratic achievement* frame, this frame proposed that the referendum would have a lasting impact on Scottish public life either way. Its indicators were references to families and groups of friends and colleagues being split over the referendum issue, and references to the referendum as being divisive or causing tensions in Scottish society.

Whereas the *policy* frame was a very pragmatic representation of what the referendum was about, all the issue-specific frames presented above were symbolic frames, namely frames focusing on symbolic, cultural meanings and social values (Castelló and Capdevila, 2013). The differences in how the referendum was understood by each of these frames led to the decision to conceptualise them separately in this analysis. As will be seen later in this chapter, symbolic frames were not particularly prominent in the referendum coverage, even if they were to be taken together as one category. This is in contrast to mediated debates on self-determination in other national contexts, such as Catalonia (Castelló and Capdevila, 2013), for instance, where symbolic frames are more central in how independence is talked about, perhaps due to the different history of independence movements in the two contexts.

The media sample

The Scottish referendum of September 2014 was a major issue that attracted large amounts of coverage in the media even before the date of the vote was known. As discussed in chapter 2, the campaign was the longest campaign before any vote in the UK. In January 2012, Prime Minster David Cameron stated that he was prepared to agree for the referendum to take place, and that prompted the media to start debate around the issue. The debate intensified when the two official campaigns formed in spring and early summer of the same year, and especially after the official agreement between the Scottish and UK governments for the referendum to take place was signed in October 2012. Key events, such as the publication of the Scottish government's White Paper on independence in November 2013, took place almost a year before the vote. By the time the official campaign period started, four months before the date of the referendum, the actual campaign debate was well under way.

That said, the final month of any political campaign is regarded as the most significant time in shaping opinions (de Vreese and Semetko, 2004: 712) and as 'the crucial phase' (Hanggli and Kriesi, 2010) of referendums in different national contexts. Interest in the campaign is also expected to peak in the media during this time. Indeed, BBC Scotland and STV, the two main broadcasters that provide dedicated coverage for Scottish audiences, broadcast sixty-four hours of news and current affairs coverage on the referendum between 18 August and 18 September 2014, excluding any programming made for audiences in the rest of the UK. This was the main sample for the broadcast component of this content analysis and it included the early evening Scottish news bulletins (BBC's *Reporting Scotland* and *STV News at Six*), the two channels' daily Scottish current affairs programmes (*Scotland 2014* and *Scotland Tonight*) as well as any special programmes and political debates about the referendum broadcast in that period. The study focused exclusively on coverage made for audiences in Scotland because this was the electorate that would be participating in the vote. Even though UK-wide, network BBC and ITV coverage is also shown in Scotland, this is not made with the Scottish audience in mind but is tailored to a UK-wide viewership that was not directly involved in the referendum.

In the final month some of the regular news programmes extended their duration from thirty minutes to one hour and several one-off special programmes and debates about the referendum were shown, considerably more than in previous months. Interest in the referendum among audiences also peaked in that time with BBC Scotland recording up to one million Scottish viewers for its televised debates. Both in terms of volume of coverage and viewership figures the final month of the campaign provided the richest material for the television analysis. All the programmes were therefore recorded as they were being broadcast and included in the analysis.

In addition to this, BBC Scotland provided recordings from its archive of one week's coverage from September 2013, exactly one year before the referendum, so that a comparison could be drawn with an earlier key moment in the campaign. Scottish broadcasters' Scottish coverage is not available on any publicly accessible database retrospectively, but broadcasters maintain their own archives. STV did not provide comparable recordings.

Newspaper coverage allows more flexibility in sampling as it remains publicly available long after its publication. The newspaper component of the content analysis explored how the referendum was framed in a range of Scottish titles at selected moments in the two-year campaign. These titles include Scottish indigenous daily morning titles which are marketed as Scottish nationals (the *Scotsman*, the *Herald* and the *Daily Record*), their Sunday equivalents (*Scotland on Sunday*, *Sunday Herald* and *Sunday Mail*), the two Scottish editions of English newspapers (the *Scottish Sun* and the *Scottish Daily Mail*) with the highest circulations at the time of the campaign (www.abc.org.uk) and their Sunday equivalents (*Scottish Sun on Sunday* and *Scottish Mail on Sunday*). The role of these titles in the Scottish public sphere was examined in more detail in chapter 2. As noted there, the indigenous Scottish press is produced for an almost exclusively Scottish readership, but the titles are in most cases owned by non-Scottish companies; whereas the Scottish editions of UK titles only have part of their content produced for Scottish readers. Hard copies of these papers were accessed at the National Library of Scotland and all articles about the referendum in the selected weeks were included in the sample.

All these newspapers saw substantial readership losses in the years leading up to the referendum (Dekavalla, 2016) and there has been considerable debate regarding their future sustainability. Whereas as recently as 2004, Scottish tabloid titles like the *Scottish Sun* and the *Daily Record* sold about 400–500,000 copies (McNair *et al.*, 2010), by 2014 their circulations had dropped to a maximum of 200,000 copies. Broadsheet titles like the *Herald* and the *Scotsman* were in a worse situation, dropping from 70–80,000 copies in 2004 to 25–38,000 in 2014. As discussed in chapter 2, this was partly due to a general trend that saw the print press decline in the Western world, but in Scotland it was precipitated by a very competitive market where a large number of titles contested a rather small readership.

In any case, at the time of the Scottish referendum the ten newspapers studied here had a combined circulation of 1,162,352 (www.abc.org.uk data for August 2014). Considering that Scotland has a population of

5,000,000, this suggests that, despite the decline, these titles still maintained a strong position in the market. Moreover, as argued in chapter 2, newspapers continued to play an important role in the public sphere by making frames and issues available for debate, which were then picked up by other platforms.

The sample selected includes broadsheets, middle markets and tabloids (these terms denote here type of content rather than paper size), which are associated with right-of-centre (the *Scotsman*, the *Scottish Sun*, the *Scottish Daily Mail* and their Sunday editions) and left-of-centre (the *Herald*, the *Daily Record* and their Sunday editions) positions (Hutchison, 2008), even though they vary as to the degree of support each has traditionally provided to individual parties. For instance, the *Scottish Mail* and the *Daily Record* have long been very consistent in their support for the Conservatives and Labour respectively, but the other titles have varied their previous alliances. As explained in chapter 2, in past elections some of these titles lent their support to the SNP, but none of them ever endorsed independence, except the *Sunday Herald*, which came out for the Yes campaign during the final stages of the referendum.

Seven weeks were selected at different key moments in the two-year campaign to form a picture of how the newspaper coverage developed over time. These weeks cover campaign initiatives of both sides (the launch of the White Paper and the meeting of the Westminster Cabinet in Aberdeen to discuss North Sea oil); the immediate aftermath of the European parliamentary election, the only election that took place during the referendum campaign; moments when the referendum would be expected to be topical because of their timing (one year before the vote, the week of the vote and the week of one of the two televised leader debates) and a week when nothing special happened in the campaign.

At some of these periods (weeks 3 and 4) newspapers might be expected to focus more on issues promoted by each campaign (two of these were included to maintain balance between Yes and No initiatives) and week 6 may be expected to focus on political leaders' performance in the televised debate, but no such assumptions could be made for the other weeks. A total of 3,415 articles were analysed across the seven weeks and the ten outlets, with 55 per cent of them found in the four broadsheet titles. All categories of coverage were included (news, features, editorials, readers' letters and opinion articles, the latter also including articles by politicians, campaigners and members of the political commentariat), because coding focused on the themes that framed the debate rather than individual writers' points of view on these themes.

The unit of analysis was the article for the newspaper coverage and the news or current affairs item for television. Each unit was coded for

Table I Newspaper sample

Week 1	15–21 April 2013	Early week in the campaign when nothing specific happened
Week 2	16–22 September 2013	One year before the referendum
Week 3	25 November to 1 December 2013	Publication of SNP's White Paper
Week 4	24 February to 2 March 2014	UK Cabinet in Scotland to discuss independence and North Sea oil
Week 5	26 May to 1 June 2014	Week after European election, start of formal referendum campaign period
Week 6	4–10 August 2014	First televised referendum leaders' debate on 5 August
Week 7	14–20 September 2014	Week of the referendum vote

presence or absence of the different frames (Aalberg *et al.*, 2012: 169) using the indicators outlined at the start of this chapter. When an item included more than one frame, all frames present were recorded, but each was only recorded once per item. Frames were therefore not treated as mutually exclusive and could co-exist in the same narrative.

As explained earlier, some frames were used by both sides (e.g. the *policy* frame), some were 'owned' by one of the sides (e.g. *self-determination*, which was a Yes frame) and some did not favour either side (e.g. *strategic game*). However, the purpose of the study was not to examine whether the way frames were used in individual items favoured either outcome. Frames were just recorded as being present or absent, in order to identify how the media defined what the referendum was about. Ten per cent of the television sample (6.4 of the total 64 hours of coverage) was also coded by two research students. Krippendorff's alpha showed satisfactory reliability for all the different frames (ranging between $a = 0.69$ and $a = 0.85$).

The different media outlets analysed dedicated varying amounts of coverage to the referendum in the periods studied. Of the sixty-four hours of coverage recorded on the two Scottish television channels in the final month, forty-four hours were on BBC Scotland and twenty on STV. The *Scotsman* and the *Herald* had over 800 referendum articles each during the seven weeks studied, while the *Scottish Sun* had only 384. These differences are due to the varying degrees of investment by different media in Scottish coverage in general, and the available space/slots on each outlet for Scottish political news. These restrictions are not specific to the referendum: tabloid newspapers, for instance, consistently dedicate less space to political coverage than broadsheets. Despite these differences in the amount of their coverage, all the outlets studied used the same frames to discuss the referendum. The relative prominence of these frames in different media will be presented subsequently in order to explore how each platform defined what the 2014 referendum was about.

A game of strategy

The *strategic game* frame was very prominent throughout the newspaper and television sample, as might be expected from the previous studies on elections and referendums reviewed in chapter 1. In the press, it was present in 1,803 articles (53 per cent of the total coverage) across the different papers, making it the most prominent frame overall. Similarly on television, it was again the most prominent frame, represented in 70 per cent of BBC Scotland and 69 per cent of STV coverage in the final month.

In both media platforms, the *game* frame became most prominent at the end of the campaign. In newspapers it was consistently the second most prominent frame in the first five weeks studied (sampled between April 2013 and June 2014) and it was only in the last two weeks of the sample (in August and September 2014) that it became the primary way of defining the referendum. Figure 1 shows how prominent the different frames measured were in different weeks across all the titles in the newspaper sample. The prominence individual newspapers gave to these frames will be explored in a later section of this chapter. As the television sampling period was a single block of one month, figure 2 shows the prominence of different frames by channel analysed.

Although the television sample was based on the final stage of the referendum campaign, as explained earlier, BBC Scotland provided archival coverage of the week the White Paper on independence was published, in September 2013 (16–22 September 2013), and analysis of that week's BBC Scotland coverage revealed that the *game* frame was second in prominence, following the *policy* frame, exactly as was the case with the press sample in the same week.

These findings are consistent with previous studies exploring the appearance of the *strategic game* frame in various election and referendum campaigns in different contexts. The *game* frame is particularly common in American presidential election coverage, for example, where it has been found to dominate between 40 and 70 per cent of the news in different studies (Iyengar *et al.*, 2004), but it is also common in referendum campaigns in Europe and in Canada (Robinson, 1998; de Vreese

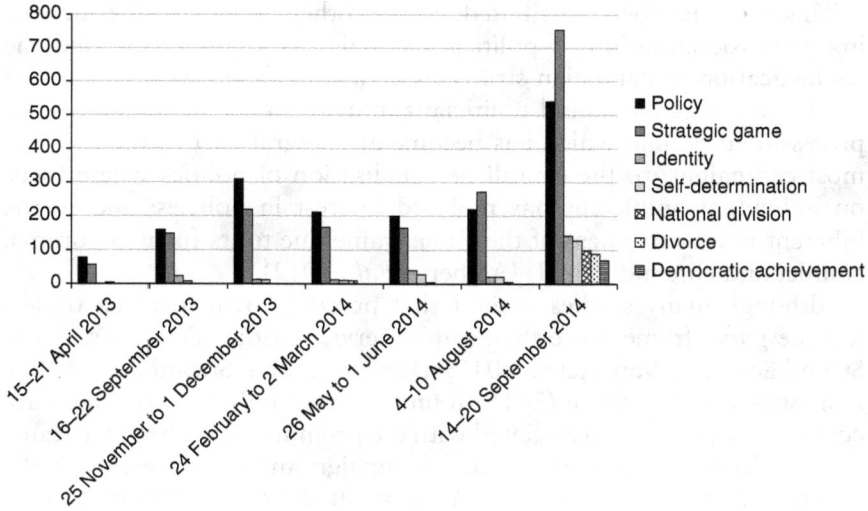

Figure 1 Prominence of frames in newspapers per week (total number of articles)

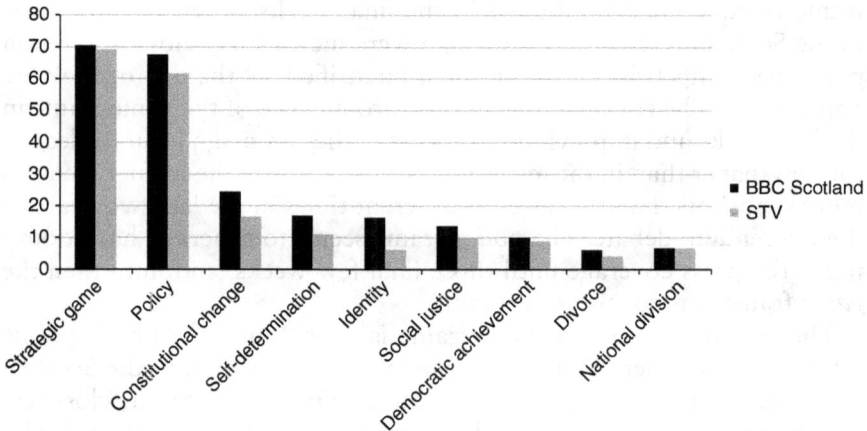

Figure 2 Prominence of frames on BBC Scotland and STV coverage between 18 August and 18 September 2014 (percentage of each channel's coverage)

and Semetko, 2004), as was seen in previous chapters. The findings of the analysis of the Scottish referendum coverage therefore are consistent with a trend identified in many other countries (Strömbäck and Kaid, 2008) of representing political campaigns to a great extent as competitions between opponents.

This trend has been attributed, among other factors, to the increasing professionalisation of political campaign communication and the sophistication of campaign strategies, which push journalists to reflect on the motivations behind politicians' moves; to the increasing use of professional polling which has become an integral part of reporting in most campaigns; to the overall personalisation of politics where focus on individual politicians has replaced interest in policies; and to the inherent newsworthiness of the *game* frame due to its focus on drama, conflict and elite individuals (Aalberg *et al.*, 2012).

Although many studies suggest that privately owned media outlets use the *game* frame more than public service media (Dunaway, 2008; Strömbäck and Van Aelst, 2010; Dimitrova and Strömbäck, 2011), Dunaway and Lawrence (2015) found that the only factors which are consistently positively associated with the prominence of the *game* frame are the degree of competition in a campaign and the closeness of the coverage to the day of the vote. As they put it, 'ownership structure ... does not trump journalists' (and audiences') attraction to the horse race when a close race is on' (Dunaway and Lawrence, 2015: 56).

Their findings resonate with the analysis presented here: the *game* frame became most prominent in the final weeks, when the two sides in the Scottish referendum campaign were increasingly close in opinion polls and competition between them intensified, as the day of the vote approached. The contrast between the prominence of the game frame in the last weeks and in previous moments in the campaign is more clear in the newspaper than in the television sample, because the former includes more snapshots than the latter of different times in the last two years of the referendum debate. The *policy* frame seems to generally have dominated the press coverage until those final few weeks, and until then the *game* frame was consistently second.

The prominence of the *game* frame is consistent across both public service and commercial media in the sample. Therefore, in the Scottish case too, as suggested by Dunaway and Lawrence (2015), the closeness of the contest and the timeliness of the vote seem the most likely explanations for the increased use of the *strategic game* frame at the end of the campaign, rather than the different media's ownership status.

Apart presenting quantitative evidence though, which involves measuring the presence of the *strategic game* frame and testing associations with factors like ownership status or closeness of election date, previous studies have not so far explored with journalists themselves how they experience the *game* frame and what factors in their daily reporting might give it particular prominence.

Quantitative evidence certainly has contributed majorly to our understanding of how measurable factors such as the ones mentioned so far might correlate with the appearance of the *game* frame, but this would be usefully complemented with insights of the way personal, organisational, media and extra-media elements in daily journalistic practices impact on this framing. Chapter 5 will address this aspect by focusing particularly on the television coverage and exploring the reasons that gave prominence to this frame according to the accounts of the broadcasters who were directly involved in reporting on the campaign at BBC Scotland and STV.

A decision about policy

As shown in Figure 1, the press framed the referendum as being about *policy* for most of the campaign (in total the frame was present in 1,735 articles, or 51 per cent of the total coverage), except for the final weeks. Even when the *strategic game* frame took over near the end, *policy* was still the second most prominent frame in newspapers. The same pattern between the two frames was also found on television in the final month, when the *policy* frame was present in 68 per cent of the BBC and 62 per cent of the STV coverage (versus 70 per cent and 69 per cent respectively for the *strategic game* frame – figure 2). As explained in the previous section, this shift of attention from *policy* to *strategic game* as the referendum approached is likely due to the increased competition between the two sides, and to the predicted closeness of the outcome towards the end.

A range of interconnected policy areas were linked to the referendum decision under the *policy* frame. Overall the frame proposed that deciding whether or not Scotland would become independent should be based on which outcome voters believed would result in better management of different areas of the economy (such as trade, business investment, currency, jobs, pensions, oil reserves, taxation and national debt), public services (mostly healthcare and education), welfare, membership of international alliances (mainly the EU and NATO), borders and immigration, defence (including the military but also the future of the Trident nuclear deterrent on the west coast of Scotland), law and order, arts and the media, and childcare.

Depending on whether the frame was used by the Yes or the No camp, existing arrangements in these areas were constructed as problematic or advantageous, and the referendum was constructed as an opportunity to change them for the better or to secure them from being lost. Clearly economic aspects are directly or indirectly connected to decisions in all other policy areas, and the economic policy consequences of the referendum were particularly prominent within the frame as they are in most political contests (de Vreese *et al.*, 2001).

However, strictly speaking, the question set on the ballot paper did not involve specific policy outcomes. These depend on the proposals of election candidates, the outcomes of elections, and the future, and often unpredictable, circumstances in which governments would be required to make decisions. Framing the referendum as being about *policy* logically promotes an expectation that specific policy outcomes would be delivered as a result of a No or a Yes vote, in the same way that voters would expect such outcomes to be delivered after an election.

As will be discussed in the concluding chapter, the 2016 UK referendum on EU membership was also framed as a decision on policy, primarily immigration policy and investment in healthcare. In the aftermath of that vote, however, the gap between promises made during the campaign in relation to reducing immigration and increasing healthcare investment, and what may be possible to deliver as a result of a vote for Britain to leave the EU, appears greater than might have been originally suggested during the campaign. Similarly, the argument of the Better Together campaign in the 2014 Scottish referendum that the only way to protect Scotland's continued membership of the EU would be to stay in the UK also appears dubious in the aftermath of 2016. This points to the problematic nature of connecting specific policy outcomes with the outcome referendums on issues which are much broader than individual policies.

Tierney (2012: 228) suggests that even when the questions on referendum ballot papers are clear, confusion may be introduced when there are 'unpredictable political contingencies' in the implementation of what is being proposed. I would argue that this is even more the case when what is being proposed (independence or status quo) is reconstructed as a set of proposals (financial security, strong currency, protection of the NHS or free childcare), which depend on even more contingencies than just the electorate voting Yes or No to constitutional change.

In both the Scottish and the EU referendums, policy outcomes were tied to a decision on constitutional status. Although the *policy* frame may indeed translate into 'substantive' media coverage (as explained in chapter 1) because it means that 'issues' are being discussed in the media rather than the process of the campaign, this does not necessarily entail that the *policy* frame is always unproblematic in the context of a national referendum because policy is not always the issue being decided on.

That said, as argued in chapters 2 and 3, the *policy* frame appears somehow inevitable in the Scottish referendum case. Much of the Scottish autonomy debate was historically connected to practical governance issues (Paterson, 2015) and both Yes Scotland and Better Together, each for their own reasons as seen in chapter 3, decided to use this frame in their media communications. The next chapter shall discuss a range of reasons why television journalists also adopted this frame and used it almost as much as the *strategic game* frame in their media accounts.

As discussed in chapter 3, the *policy* frame also featured very prominently in public opinion, as this was manifested both in opinion polls (TNS-BMRB, 2014) and in Twitter discussions (Fang *et al.*, 2015; Quinlan *et al.*, 2015). However, due to reasons examined in that chapter, it is difficult to establish, the extent to which similarities between audience frames and media frames are the direct result of framing effects from the campaigns and the media to the public. This question lies beyond the scope of the present research and would require different methods to explore it. In a debate that is as historically entrenched as the Scottish independence issue (as explained in chapter 2), it is indeed very complicated to prove uni-directional framing effects, because the public came to the 2014 campaign with historical preconceptions, which were in turn drawn upon by the Yes and No camps when creating their communication messages.

This latter point also justifies the relative absence of symbolic frames both from the campaign messages and the media coverage, as will be discussed below.

A decision based on values

All the 'symbolic' frames (Castelló and Capdevila, 2013) presented at the start of this chapter enjoyed considerably less prominence in the coverage of both print and television outlets. In the press, symbolic frames received more mentions in the final week compared to previous periods, as interest in the referendum peaked towards the end (figure 1), but even then they lagged behind the two dominant frames discussed so far. This was also the case on television (figure 2).

Even if all symbolic frames were to be added together, one or more symbolic frames appeared in 45 per cent of the BBC coverage and 37 per cent of the STV coverage in the final month, which still suggests that as a broader category they were not as prominent as the pragmatic implications or the game of the campaign, whose presence in the television coverage was between 60 and 70 per cent (figure 2).

Moreover, in the press coverage only *national identity* and *self-determination* received any attention (even if little) in the weeks of the newspaper sample before the very end of the campaign. The other symbolic frames only emerged in the final week of that sample, suggesting that symbolic frames were not as prominent in the debate during the earlier stages of the campaign. On the other hand, perhaps because the television sample focused on the final four weeks, all the different symbolic frames were present throughout it.

This may seem surprising in a referendum on national independence, but pragmatic considerations have long been central in debates around Scottish autonomy. A frame analysis of Scottish and English newspaper coverage on the issue of independence during the 2007 Scottish election found a balance between symbolic and pragmatic frames (Castelló and Capdevila, 2013), where independence was talked about as much in terms of what the present study has defined as the *identity* and *divorce* frames, as it was in terms of the *policy* frame. This lends support to the argument of this book that the discussion of Scottish independence in pragmatic *policy* terms has roots that go further in the past than the coverage of the 2014 referendum itself.

Finally *democratic achievement* and *national division*, the two 'neutral' frames which were not promoted by either political side, had very marginal presence in newspapers and television alike, suggesting that non-partisan frames that did not enjoy elite sponsorship did not have much resonance in the media. Journalists, as will be seen in more detail in chapter 5, mainly used the frames proposed by elite political sources and did not introduce any prominent frames of their own other than the *strategic game* frame.

Having looked at overall patterns in how newspapers and television framed the coverage, I will now to turn to explore whether there were similarities or differences in the framing between individual newspaper or television outlets.

The framing of the referendum in individual outlets

The prominence that the different media included in this study gave to each frame is surprisingly similar, considering that the sample was made up of a wide diversity of outlets, namely commercial, public service, left and right of centre, politically neutral, broadsheet and tabloid, with and without links to larger London media. All these differentiating factors might have been expected to lead to differences in the framing of the referendum in the coverage, but this was not the case.

The relative prominence of the frames in the different newspaper titles studied was very much homogeneous: as can be seen in table 2, the *game* and *policy* frames competed closely in most papers, each being present in around half of their coverage. There are just a couple of exceptions to this pattern: in the daily and Sunday edition of the *Scottish Sun* and in the *Sunday Mail* (but not in its daily equivalent, the *Daily Record*) the *game* frame was dominant over *policy* by a larger margin compared to the other newspapers. This seems broadly in line with research indicating

Table 2 Distribution of frames: percentage of overall referendum coverage per newspaper

	Policy	Strategic game	Identity	Divorce	Democratic achievement	Self-determination	National division
Scotsman	54.3	43.8	8.3	1.4	0.6	6.5	3.5
Herald	50.8	53.8	5.1	2.6	3.2	4.5	2.4
Daily Record	47.6	51.1	5.8	3	3.2	7	3.4
Scottish Sun	39	65.4	6.5	2.9	2.3	6.5	2.9
Scottish Daily Mail	52.2	57.3	11.9	5.1	1.7	4.2	6.6
Scotland on Sunday	75.5	50	8.8	0	0	6.8	1.9
Sunday Herald	56.3	55.5	6.7	2.5	3.4	10.1	0.8
Sunday Mail	42.7	57.3	4.9	0	2.4	11	1.2
Scottish Sun on Sunday	48.7	56.4	15.4	0	0	10.2	5.1
Scottish Mail on Sunday	50.6	51.8	8.4	4.8	0	6	3.6

that contest frames are more common in tabloid than broadsheet news-papers (Gerth and Siegert, 2012). On the other hand, the *Scotsman* and its Sunday sister *Scotland on Sunday* were the only titles where the *policy* frame was overall more prominent than the *game* frame.

As shown in figure 2, the *policy* and *game* frames also competed very closely on television: on BBC Scotland the balance was 70 per cent for the *game* frame and 68 per cent for *policy*, while on STV 69 per cent of the coverage included the *game* frame and 62 per cent the *policy* frame. Symbolic frames appear to be better represented on television than in newspapers, with several of them present in between 10 per cent and 23 per cent of individual channels' coverage, and none of them falling below 3 per cent of the broadcast coverage (whereas in many newspaper titles some symbolic frames were present in as little as 0–0.8 per cent of the coverage, as shown in table 2). Still, the differences in the timing of the samples used for television and newspapers do not allow a more direct comparison between the two platforms.

One pattern, however, does emerge clearly from the content analysis of the referendum coverage on different media: despite small differences between individual outlets, the broader picture was very similar. The *policy* and *game* frames competed closely at all stages of the campaign, and the *game* frame took over near the end, as voting day approached and the competition between the two sides increased. Even at that time though, the *policy* frame did not lose its prominence and came a close second. Symbolic frames, on the other hand, were considerably less prominent as a group. Among them, the most prominent were *identity* and *self-determination*, while *constitutional change* emerged only towards the end.

Broadcasting in the UK is required to be impartial in all political matters,[1] while newspapers are partisan and can explicitly express opinion for or against political actors and causes. This difference, however, did not necessarily alter how the debate was framed between television and the press. As mentioned in chapter 2, the different newspaper titles included in this study have very different political positions on the ideological spectrum, and the *Sunday Herald* was the only openly pro-independence mainstream news medium at the time of the campaign. Despite this, the prominence of different frames between them all was rather similar (table 2), and the *Sunday Herald*, like other newspapers and like television, had a close balance between *policy* and *game* frames, and no significant differences from officially impartial or more sceptical media in the balance between the other frames.

The arguments this newspaper provided may have been different from those found in other media (a more detailed qualitative analysis would be required to explore this), but the *Sunday Herald* did not challenge the overall consensus that the referendum was about policy and the competition between the two campaign sides. The relatively high presence of the *self-determination* frame in the *Sunday Herald* compared to its daily sister the *Herald* does not make it distinctive overall, as it was also found in other Sunday titles (*Sunday Mail* and *Scottish Sun on Sunday*) which, like the *Herald*, did not support independence (table 2).

The next chapter will seek to explain this dominance of the *policy* and *game* frames in the media. It will focus particularly on the two broadcasters analysed in the coverage sample, BBC Scotland and STV, and the factors which may have played a role in promoting these frames according to interviews with members of the news teams that covered the referendum.

Apart from the homogeneity of the framing across different media, a second significant pattern emerging from this content analysis is that the *strategic game* and *policy* frames were not mutually exclusive in the coverage. Despite the fact that they are often seen in the literature as opposites (Robinson, 1998; Lawrence, 2000; Iyengar *et al.*, 2004), at least in normative terms as explained in chapter 1, in all the media sampled here they often appeared together within the same stories. For example, in the television coverage of the final month of the campaign across both channels, 62 per cent of news and current affairs items that contained the *strategic game* frame also included the *policy* frame, even though the association between the two was not exactly statistically significant ($p = 0.9$).

This suggests that the two frames can often co-exist and complement each other (although they don't necessarily always do, as suggested by the statistical significance test). As discussed in chapter 1, theorists see the *game* frame as potentially harmful for informed citizenry (Cappella and Jamieson, 1997; Robinson, 1998) because it detracts attention from reasoned debate around the 'issues' and promotes cynicism in relation to politicians and their motives. At the same time though, the performance of individual political leaders and the horserace of the campaign can attract audiences more effectively than policy debates (Iyengar *et al.*, 2004). This could be because these elements of 'horserace' and competition represent the emotional aspect of politics, which is just as important as the rational part (Verstraeten, 1996; Dahlgren, 2006).

Although the *strategic game* frame does not favour any specific referendum outcome, it too is an emotional frame, which positions voters as supporters of political 'teams', who are excited or emotionally moved by a potential victory or a defeat of their side. In one of the presentations of this research in 2015, a member of the audience suggested that if the side that they supported won the referendum that would be rewarding in itself, and that any *policy* consequences resulting from this victory would be of secondary significance, further down the line. There is of course no evidence that all audiences think this way, but this comment does reflect that there is an emotional side to elections and referendums represented by the *game* frame, whereby supporters of political parties and coalitions are interested in how the political proposal they support is performing in the 'race', how their leaders are doing in debates, and whether eventually their side is going to win. Political decisions are not exclusively about reasoned evaluation of arguments but they are also about emotional attachment to a 'team' and to political leaders as public personae and performers.

Therefore media coverage that combines the *game* frame with the *policy* frame at the same time combines what political campaigns propose around policy *as well as* a focus on how they are performing. I therefore propose that the two frames are not contradictory, but can complement each other, representing two facets of a campaign, which are interwoven in practice. As I will argue in chapter 6, journalists use the *strategic game* frame to reframe the *policy* and other advocacy frames, rather than to promote an alternative definition of what is at stake. Thus one of the advantages of coding media coverage for presence or absence of the *game* and *policy* frames, rather than attempting to assign a single frame to each story, is that such an analysis allows the researcher to capture this dual nature of news coverage.

Besides, empirical evidence has shown that although the *game* frame can lead to voter cynicism, it does not prevent voters from engaging with politics and turning out to vote (de Vreese and Semetko, 2002). Some have even suggested that learning about how different parties or political sides are doing in opinion polls can contribute to help undecided voters in making a decision when the date of the vote is approaching (Irwin and Van Holsteyn, 2008). Overall, there seems to be no evidence from a review of empirical studies that the *game* frame has a negative impact on the public (Aalberg *et al.*, 2012). The *strategic game* frame therefore may in fact support the democratic process, when combined with other more 'substantial' frames.

Of course the potential effects the *game* frame might have in public discourse or on audiences did not play any role in journalists' decision to use the *policy* and *game* frames in combination. As discussed in chapter 1, media framing is not always a conscious process and journalists draw from among frames that are culturally available and from frames promoted by their sources. The next chapter will focus particularly on how this process works. It will discuss how journalists who covered the referendum campaign framed the event on television and which factors in their daily work encouraged the prominence of the frames identified and measured in this chapter. Following this, chapter 6 will use these insights to propose a model which may account for journalistic frame-building during a referendum campaign, and which goes beyond the specific case study and could account more broadly for how the context of reporting on a highly contested referendum may be connected with the prominence of specific frames in the media output.

Note

1 During the Scottish referendum campaign broadcasters, and particularly the BBC, were accused of lack of impartiality by Yes supporters. An exploration of these claims is beyond the scope of this book.

5

The process of frame-building

How journalists frame political events in the news will vary depending on the combination of a range of possible factors specific to journalists themselves, the organisations they work for, their occupational routines, the media system, and the values held by the specific society (Shoemaker and Reese, 2014), as explained in chapter 1. The challenge for researchers 'is to identify the conditions that determine the degree of journalistic frame setting' (Brüggemann, 2014: 61), namely the degree to which journalists are likely to frame the coverage based on their own interpretations of what the event is about, rather than those of their sources.

This chapter addresses this question by identifying factors that may influence whether and how journalists use political sources' frames during a highly contested referendum campaign. As was seen in the previous two chapters, the frames that political communicators promoted in the case of the Scottish referendum also emerged in media coverage. This chapter explores the factors that may have led to their prominence on television, by analysing a set of interviews with Scottish broadcasters who covered the referendum on BBC Scotland and STV. The chapter will use the accounts of key participants in the news making process to discuss how the frames presented in previous chapters emerged in the news narratives that they created, since the only access we may have to the frame-building process is through the accounts of those directly involved in it. The chapter focuses particularly on broadcast news and current affairs coverage of the referendum, and explores which factors may explain why some frames became more prominent.

I will argue that five factors relating to occupational routines, perceptions of professionalism, institutional norms and extra-media relationships with sources – therefore a range of different levels of Shoemaker and Reese's (2014) model discussed in chapter 1 – combined to push certain frames to prominence in the television coverage. The insights from this analysis will contribute to understanding the frame-building process in other similar contexts, where journalists in liberal media systems report on highly contested referendum campaigns. Chapter 6 will propose a frame-building model, based on these insights, which may help account for this process beyond the context of the specific referendum.

The particular emphasis in this chapter is on the relative prominence of the *strategic game* and *policy* frames which, as was seen in chapters 1 and 4, were very prominent both in this and in other similar campaigns. Therefore the analysis will inform our understanding of how *game* and *policy* frames emerge and relate to each other during the coverage of a referendum and it will make a contribution to literature on these two frames, as well as to broader frame-building literature.

Brüggemann (2014: 75) suggests that the primary evidence that journalists are setting their own frames is when the frames they evoke in interviews, therefore the frames that they 'favour', are also found to be particularly dominant in content analysis of the media coverage they produced. This chapter will argue that this is not necessarily so. In a highly polarised and conflictive issue, like Scottish independence, the frames evoked by broadcast journalists in interviews were not necessarily their own 'favoured' frames, but the pressure they felt to appear impartial meant that they attributed any frames they mentioned to political sources, even during the interviews. The journalists interviewed seemed to avoid at all costs to be seen as constructing their own frames or 'favouring' any frames. This does not mean that they did not actually engage in frame-building: the *strategic game* frame is a journalistic frame that they introduced in the coverage to serve their perceptions of balance requirements and of what they felt the audience wanted to see. Thus in the case of the *strategic game* frame, frame construction is not necessarily a decision based on journalists' preferred interpretation of a news event, but a pragmatic decision based on what they perceive as serving professional and commercial/organisational standards.

Some of what will be discussed here relates only to television, given that UK broadcasting operates under different requirements of impartiality from the print press, which as explained in chapter 2 can take sides and express political opinion openly. However some of the factors identified in the interviews with broadcasters may also hold for print media. For example, the perceived effectiveness of the *strategic game* frame in attracting the attention of audiences, the high level of dependence of journalists on the formal campaigns as the main sources for their coverage, or their established familiarity with the reporting context of elections more than with that of referendums, are not unique to broadcasting but characterise all mainstream media. Arguably some of these factors are even more significant in commercial organisations, like newspapers, where there is no obligation to be balanced and more pressure to attract readers' attention in order to sell copies.

The interviewees in this chapter are television reporters and producers, political editors and heads of news and current affairs at the two television channels. They were all directly involved in the day-to-day coverage of the referendum and remained central in the reporting teams of the two broadcasters at the time when these interviews took place in the first half of 2015 – all but one were still there at the time of writing. They are experienced journalists and producers who had worked in Scottish political news for many years before the referendum. They represent key members of what is a relatively small group of Scottish television newsmakers.

The value of these interviews is the opportunity to explore the framing of the coverage of the campaign through the perspectives of those who were directly implicated in producing it. Clearly, since the research was carried out after the event, interviews represent journalists' own narratives of how they reported it rather than an outsider's observation of these processes as they happened – journalists' self-reporting on their practices may introduce a potential degree of 'subjectivity' in their accounts. Still these interviews offer considerable insight into the thinking behind the coverage and they contribute to an understanding of how journalists themselves experienced these frames and how they fitted with their day-to-day reporting of the campaign. This is a question that is rarely explored in frame analysis literature (a few other examples were reviewed in chapter 1), which works with texts but often does not consult the perspectives of their producers. Qualitative interviewing allows an in-depth exploration of interviewees' perceptions, understandings and reasoning for their actions and is based on a constructivist view of the social world, whereby accounts of events can only be constructed through the 'subjectivity' of those who participate in them (Kvale, 1996). Interviewing different participants in an event allows to explore their different perspectives, and establish patterns in the rationale that guides their actions.

The purpose of the interviews was to explore journalists' perceptions of what the referendum was about and where they thought these definitions originated; their daily work routines and how they fed into the content they produced; the process that led to editorial decision-making, particularly in relation to which stories they covered, how they determined what was at stake and who they used as their sources; as well as their perceptions of the role and obligations of television, and of their own role as reporters in the context of a major referendum. After several questions on these broader aspects referring to the specific context of the final month of the campaign, interviewees were eventually told, towards the end of the interviews, what the two main frames identified in the coverage were and were asked to comment on them.

In what follows I will explore five factors, which played a role in the framing of the campaign on television, as this was presented in chapter 4, and map these factors onto Shoemaker and Reese's (2014) model of factors influencing news content. As discussed in chapter 1, this model was not meant to account for framing specifically but for all kinds of impacts on journalistic content. Still it offers a very useful conceptual framework that can help structure an account of what shapes the frames that we find in the news, even though in reality factors at different analytical levels interact with each other.

This chapter will propose that the *policy* frame was promoted in the coverage by the heavy reliance of journalists on the two official campaigns, who both communicated this frame as was seen in chapter 3; this is an extra-media factor relating to the relationship between the media and organisations and institutions outside the media (Shoemaker and Reese, 2014). Another factor that contributed to the *policy* frame becoming so dominant was journalists' own perception of their role in the coverage of the campaign, a factor relating to personal role perceptions and values. On the other hand, three factors promoted the *strategic game* frame: the influence of the balance ritual, a factor relating to occupation routines; broadcasters' institutional perceptions of what attracts audiences, which is a factor relating to organisational influences; and journalists' previous experience of covering election campaigns, a factor at the individual level of the influence model (Shoemaker and Reese, 2014). In the rest of this chapter, I will explain and substantiate each of these factors with evidence from the interviews.

How journalists were told what the referendum was about: the influence of official campaigns

At the extra-media level of influences to journalistic content (Shoemaker and Reese, 2014) the two official campaigns were found to have a major role in framing the news coverage.

When asked to provide their personal 'favoured' frames during the interviews, by answering the question 'in your mind, what was the referendum about?' members of the two television news teams hesitated to give their own definitions. Some interviewees repeated the question on the ballot paper ('should Scotland be an independent country') or slightly paraphrased it (e.g. 'the future course Scotland would take'). Journalists seemed reluctant to mention specific frames, and when they did, they attributed them to the campaigns. For example:

> I suppose the Yes side boiled it down to a matter of democracy, that if you had an independent country, you would always get the governments that you voted for was one of their core lines ... And then on the other side, I think it was core to their argument that you could have better change within the United Kingdom, more powers within the UK, while still benefiting from the strengths of the UK.

The interviewee here proposes two of the frames seen in chapter 3, namely the *self-determination* frame ('if you had an independent country, you would always get the governments that you voted for') and the *constitutional change* frame ('you could have better change within the United Kingdom, more powers within the UK') and attributes each frame to the campaign that sponsored it.

Another journalist acknowledged that the referendum question was reframed during the campaign:

> although the way the debate was framed in the build-up, the question was 'should Scotland be an independent country', the debate moved beyond that into 'what kind of country do you want to live in' ... it became a very fundamental discussion about what values you want to see in your country for education, the health service, immigration, role in the world and in Europe.

Some interviewees argued that this reframing of the debate from a purely constitutional decision to one about policy areas like 'education, the health service, immigration, role in the world and in Europe' (in other words the promotion of the *policy* frame as a definition of what the debate was about) was done by the public. Indeed the interviewee quoted directly above later in the interview said that he thought that this framing was driven by the grassroots level, by communities and ordinary people. However most of the interviewees attributed the *policy* frame to the official campaigns. For example:

> a lot of these assertions were made by each campaign, but it is true to say that, and actually a politician did admit this, that, you know, we don't know in detail how things would work in an independent Scotland, which policies would be pursued because there'd be a general election in an independent Scotland. Having said that, it's obvious that the SNP's prospectus, the White Paper, was very policy-driven.

> The Yes campaign had themselves tried to focus so much of the attention for the debate not on any kind of cultural or ethnic nationalism, but on economic opportunities for Scotland, that would be available if Scotland

were independent. And as a result, I think, of their determination to focus on the economics, there was also a commensurate focus on critiquing the economics and that followed.

I think probably the campaigns shaped the agenda more than broadcasters did.

The above three quotes each come from a different interviewee, and these respondents are from both BBC Scotland and STV. All three agree that the political campaigns determined what the referendum was about, and particularly chose to focus on policy.

Indeed, the first two interviewees quoted seem to attribute the *policy* frame to the Yes campaign. As discussed in chapter 3, the Yes campaign did have a strategy of promoting policy issues, most explicitly in the Scottish government's 2013 White Paper on independence, because its strategists believed that defining the decision as being about policy would engage voters in the debate. However, the Yes campaign was certainly not the only side promoting this frame, as explained in that chapter. The key messages of the No campaign also focused on policy areas, and particularly on economic policy, and this decision was based on Better Together's own polling. As discussed in chapter 3, this was not simply a reaction to Yes Scotland's framing. Still the above interviewees' perception seems to be that not only the campaigns led the framing of the debate, but also that the Yes campaign was responsible for the prominence of the *policy* frame.

Another related point that emerged very clearly from all the interviews with broadcasters was that the two official campaigns were the primary sources used in the day-to-day coverage of the referendum, especially towards the end. This is consistent with the interviewees' view above that the campaigns framed the referendum: their privileged access to the media meant that they had more opportunities to promote their frames, and particularly the *policy* frame, which was promoted by both camps. Although all interviewees pointed out that their channels made their own independent decisions on what to cover and also produced original material, in practice towards the end of the campaign period the two official campaigns had a central role in television's everyday coverage.

Asked about their main sources in the coverage of the referendum, one interviewee suggested that:

in news you are driven to a degree by events that the organisations stage and hold, you obviously look at issues that you think are important, but you can't ignore the news of the day. And the news of the day is often what people decide to do – initiatives, press conferences, launches and so on.

Considering that Yes Scotland and Better Together were formally designated as the 'official' campaigns promoting each outcome, and they were
also made up of powerful political parties and high-profile social actors
who already enjoyed elite status in the public sphere before the referendum, it is not surprising that they became the first point of contact for
journalists' day-to-day coverage. Their status made them newsworthy.
As two other interviewees proposed, when asked what kind of features
would guarantee coverage for a referendum-related story:

> if you've got particularly big hitters, if you like, entering the campaign,
> especially if it's for the first time, if there's something new about either
> the fact that they are getting involved, or what it is that they've got to
> say ... then these might be factors that would make you think, that's
> quite newsy.

> I would say that pronouncements by the actors, the main actors, the main
> politicians involved were the main source of stories. So if Alex Salmond for
> the Scottish National Party was saying something or if the prime minister
> was saying something, that would naturally carry a certain weight.

Elite status, or being a 'big hitter' as the first interviewee above puts it,
is a well-established criterion in journalistic news values (Harcup and
O'Neil, 2001). Just the fact that a 'big hitter' makes a statement about
the referendum is newsworthy in itself. The combination of elite status
(being a well-known social actor) and official status (representing the
official views of a major organisation) meant that the two campaigns
had excellent access and the opportunity to frame the debate. This access
was embedded in day-to-day practices at the television channels. As the
interviewee below says, even the structure of their reporting teams was
shaped to follow the two official campaigns:

> I would follow essentially the Yes campaign, with a cameraman and edi-
> tor – we have what we call a shoot-edit, someone who films and edits as
> well – so a senior cameraman who would also do the editing, the pic-
> ture editing, so it would be me, a cameraman and editor, and a produ-
> cer as a core team following the Yes campaign. And there was a parallel
> team following the No campaign. The idea was that we would follow both
> campaigns and we would try to report on, you know, to reflect what was
> happening on the ground with both campaigns.

The organisation of daily reporting that the interviewee describes illus-
trates the power of the campaigns in the coverage. Other actors may have
had the opportunity to influence the debate by sending press releases and
inviting journalists to their events, as indeed many civil society organisations did (as discussed in chapter 3), however these actors did not have

their own dedicated reporting team at the channels. The structure of working routines inside the channels was shaped by the central role they gave to the official campaigns. Two interviewees pointed out that the practical logistics required for television to cover any event, particularly in terms getting a crew at a location to film, meant that television was more restricted than other media in what it could cover without advance planning. The division of labour described above may have been meant to address these restrictions by making a crew available to report on each official campaign on a regular basis, however at the same time it also constitutes an editorial decision on who are seen as the most important sources who would determine the framing of the event, and where significant action is expected to take place. Indeed, in the final month of the coverage 47 per cent of the sources that appeared on BBC Scotland's daily news bulletin were politicians, and 60 per cent were more broadly elite official sources; the remaining 40 per cent were grassroots campaigners, small businesses and unions, experts and ordinary citizens all taken together (Dekavalla and Jelen-Sanchez, 2016).

Clearly it is not practically easy to exclude politicians from a referendum debate. Issues are not put to the public vote because politicians are indifferent to them; on the contrary highly politically charged issues, like independence in this case, are the ones that tend to be decided by referendums. Even if politicians had stayed out of the media debate themselves, the grassroots campaigns promoting both sides of the argument in 2014 were still nurtured by the official political campaigns, so the influence of the latter would have remained.

Perhaps, though, as one of the few occasions of direct democracy that most citizens will experience in their lifetime, referendums offer an opportunity to reverse the usual order that puts elite media sources first and to provide more examples of citizens debating public affairs, from a partisan but also from a non-partisan perspective. This opportunity was taken but only to a restricted degree compared to the centrality of official sources. The broadcasters interviewed stressed that they made a conscious effort to include a range of sources in their coverage but, as explained above, the majority of sources were still elite officials (Dekavalla and Jelen-Sanchez, 2016).

Their role as central sources meant not only that the two campaigns had significant airtime at their disposal to promote their frames, but also that they enjoyed a 'primary definer' role (Hall et al., 1978) in determining what the debate was about. This is in line with suggestions that political elites are influential in frame-building (Brewer and Gross, 2010; Gerth and Siegert, 2012; Hanggli, 2012). However the findings from the present research additionally suggest that those frames which are simultaneously contested by more than one elite group (in the Scottish case the *policy* frame) are more likely to be prominent in the news than frames which are promoted by one side. This is an issue that previous research on referendums has not highlighted because in most studies different sides were found to promote contrasting frames. Indeed both campaigns in the Scottish referendum also had a range of other messages that framed the referendum in symbolic terms as well as in pragmatic terms, as discussed in chapter 3. However the *policy* frame was claimed by both sides and perhaps for this reason it received the most media attention among all the frames that the two campaigns promoted.

Reporters questioned campaign sources on the specifics of their policy claims and, as will be discussed later in this chapter, broadcasters actively sought counter-claims to include in their coverage. Still, they did not question that the referendum was about *policy* decisions and not about *identity* for instance. In the interviews they appeared convinced that what they gave prominence to in their reports was what their viewers needed to know in order to make a decision. For example, one interviewee suggested:

> I think that what it all boils down to is do people want to ... will this help people make their decision, one way or the other? And that I think was what informed what became the big story of the day. Was it something that helped the voters, for me.

This statement would imply that broadcasters accepted that the two sides' claims on *policy* was what voters should think about in order to decide how to vote on Scottish independence. Considering all the possible frames presented in chapter 3 though, a *policy* decision was just one way of understanding the vote and choosing this frame promoted a specific ideological construction of the event as a pragmatic decision about concrete policy outcomes. As discussed in that chapter, the *policy* frame might logically lead voters to expect certain policy outcomes to result from their vote for or against independence, but this would also be problematic. As another interviewee put it:

> I mean the problem with that though is that it's a decision about the constitution. I mean I think this is part of the problem with why it was harder sometimes to get into the policy argument. Because if you were discussing policy on the NHS, what are we talking about here? Are we talking about the Scottish National Party's policy for the future of the NHS versus what? You know, versus the Labour policy, which they would argue is different from the Conservative policy or versus the Liberal Democrat policy or versus any other policy, or in fact for that matter?

Apart from the fact that the campaigns were made up of parties with often contrasting policy proposals that could lead to completely different decisions if different parties came into power, which is highlighted by the interviewee above, other factors outside the control of any of the parties could determine policy in the UK or in Scotland (as indeed happened with continued membership of the EU, following Scotland's decision to stay in the UK). Policy proposals are usually set for the public vote in elections, where voters can revise their decisions in the next electoral term. Arguably a decision on national independence was not only a longer-term decision compared to an election, but also a more abstract one, and the attempt to frame it as something very concrete with specific implications for policy-making was also potentially problematic.

This section has argued that the focus of television on the *policy* frame (and to a lesser extent on the other symbolic frames promoted by each side, such as *self-determination, divorce* or *constitutional change*) was partly due to the high level of influence both Better Together and Yes Scotland enjoyed in the mediated debate. This is an extra-media influencing factor on journalistic content (Shoemaker and Reese, 2014). The reason why, among the different frames the two sides promoted, the pragmatic *policy* frame received more attention seems to be that it was contested by both camps. Although previous research found political campaigns to also be responsible for the promotion of the *game* frame in the coverage of elections (Cushion *et al.*, 2016), this was not explicitly mentioned by any of the interviewees in the referendum context analysed here.

The influence of the two campaigns discussed in this section was also reinforced by journalists' perceptions of their own role in the referendum, as will be argued subsequently. The interviews suggest that political sources' frames became prominent not only because the campaigns had a central role in the day-to-day coverage, but additionally because journalists at the two channels believed it was not their own role to interfere with how the referendum was to be framed.

Was it for the media to say what it was all about? The influence of journalists' perception of their role in the referendum

At the individual level of influences to journalistic content (Shoemaker and Reese, 2014) the way journalists perceived their own role as 'reflecting' rather than constructing the referendum debate reinforced the influence of the campaigns in framing the referendum, which was discussed in the previous section.

A common point where most of the respondents agreed was that they did not feel it was their job to frame the referendum. As the two journalists below suggested:

> I think [our duty is] to fairly and impartially reflect both sides of the argument, but in addition to that to explain, I think, what each side is actually proposing for each of the issues they're talking about. To explain to people what those issues are and what the implications of them might be.

> We assess what the issues are, and the importance they have for voters and reflect that. ... I don't think it's for broadcasters to kind of dictate or direct. ... It's to reflect the debate in as a comprehensive, informed and impartial way as possible.

Many interviewees said that, as the second excerpt above suggests, it was not for them to 'dictate or direct' the debate. They saw the referendum debate as happening 'out there', in the public sphere, and their own role as 'reflecting' (a term used by both interviewees above) or 'explaining' it to their viewers, but not as shaping it. This self-perception of journalism's role in the referendum is consistent with traditional perceptions of journalism as a 'mirror', namely 'the work of observation, tantamount to gazing on reality or the objective happenings taking place in the real world' (Zelizer, 2005: 69), which constructs journalists as recorders rather than shapers of reality. The mirror metaphor has long been central in discourses of journalistic professionalism (Vos, 2011) and remains very prominent in the ways that journalists talk about their work. The claim to 'reflect the debate' made in the excerpts above is an instance of this exact metaphor. As Lawrence (2010) proposes, the idea of journalists actively creating frames to report on a story clashes with deeply ingrained understandings of professionalism.

Clearly the mirror metaphor is an idealistic self-perception of journalists, who actually are very much involved in constructing the events and issues they present. Any attempt to narrate social reality is a construction, irrespective of the intentions of the narrator, and the media do not just reproduce but define reality. As Hall argues, 'representation is a very different notion from that of reflection. It implies the active work of selecting and presenting, of structuring and shaping: not merely the transmitting of an already- existing meaning, but the more active labour of *making things mean*' (1982: 60).

This though does not make the mirror metaphor any less important in guiding journalists' approach to news coverage. A journalist who believes their job is to 'reflect and explain' what each side of the referendum argument has to say adopts a non-interventionist approach to their work (Hanitzsch, 2007) and would logically be expected to reproduce the frames that each side proposes (Brüggemann, 2014). As seen in chapter 4, this expectation was confirmed by the content analysis of the television coverage, which reproduced most of the frames proposed by the two campaigns in chapter 3.

Consistent with the mirror metaphor was another metaphor used by the interviewees, relating to journalists' perception of their channels' role as a 'platform' or 'forum' for debate. As the respondent below suggests:

> [Our aim in the coverage of the referendum was] to become a platform for discussion and debate. And to be at the heart of it, and to be essential viewing, on television and online, to be fair and impartial, but that would be our approach in any news coverage, but generally to be engaging, to be absolutely the forum for debate.

Skovsgaard et al. (2013) found that journalists who adhere to a 'public forum' role also tend to understand objectivity as being equivalent to balance, or as will be discussed later in this chapter, as a tool or reporting ritual aiming to achieve a 'proxy for objectivity'. Although the emphasis in the forum and platform metaphors is not on media reproducing the debate as it happens elsewhere (which is the premise of the mirror metaphor), but becoming the place where the debate actually takes place and allowing viewers access to view it, what these metaphors have in common with the perception of journalism as a mirror is the allocation of a passive, non-interventionist role to journalists (Skovsgaard et al., 2013). Platforms and forums, like mirrors, do not intervene in shaping the debates that take place on them but allow the participants of the debates to construct what they are about. Like the mirror metaphor, the platform and forum metaphors are also rather idealistic self-perceptions of broadcasters. They are both based on a view of the media as 'truthfully' transferring to their audiences competing positions in a pluralist social reality and a view of 'facts' as separable from 'opinion' (Curran et al., 1982: 16).

These role perceptions meant that broadcasters acted as 'translators' (Castelló and Montagut, 2011: 514) of the frames of each political side, rather than as 'frame setters' (Brüggemann, 2014: 64). Brüggemann (2014) proposed that there is a continuum between 'frame setting' (journalists creating their own frames to discuss an issue) and 'frame sending' (journalists reproducing the frames proposed by their sources) and in this case broadcasters were closer to the latter end of this continuum than the former, partly because they believed that this was their job.

In addition to mirroring or 'sending' (Brüggemann, 2014) political sources' frames, their role as 'translators' also involved 'a didactic role, given the sometimes incomprehensible complexity of a political situation' (Castelló and Montagut, 2011: 514), which is illustrated by the claim in the first quote above that broadcasters' job was also to 'explain' the issues. This was a claim made in several of the interviews with broadcasters. Explaining the issues however does not involve challenging campaigns' proposals of what the issues were in the first place or what the referendum decision was about, but rather just explaining what each side proposes and how reasonable, realistic or feasible these proposals seem.

This self-perception of journalists' role in the campaign encouraged the prominence of the frames promoted by the two campaigns. As argued previously, the *policy* frame was particularly prominent among the official campaign frames because it was promoted by both sides. Therefore the combination of journalistic role perceptions, explored in this section, and political sources' central position in the daily routines of reporting, discussed in the previous section, together encouraged the prominence of the *policy* frame in the television coverage. I will subsequently discuss how the *strategic game* frame emerged in this coverage, despite the fact that it was not actively promoted by either political side.

Impartiality or equivalence? The influence of balance rituals

The *strategic game* frame was promoted in the television coverage examined by a perception of journalistic objectivity and impartiality as balance, which was shared by all broadcasters interviewed. This is a factor at the occupational routines level of Shoemaker and Reese's (2014) model.

Tuchman (1972) proposes that balance is a ritual followed by journalists, a compulsive routine procedure, which does not necessarily result in objective reporting but is invoked by reporters as a strategy to deflect potential criticism of bias. This strategy consists in presenting a counter-claim by sources with opposing views for every truth claim made by a source. As Tuchman explains in relation to a fictional example:

> Presenting both truth-claim 'A' attributed to the senator and truth-claim 'B' attributed to the secretary of defense, the newsman [*sic*] may then claim he is 'objective' because he has presented 'both sides of the story' without favoring either man [*sic*] or political party. Furthermore, by presenting both truth-claims, the 'objective' reporter supposedly permits the news consumer to decide whether the senator or the secretary is 'telling the truth'. (1972: 665)

Tuchman suggests that this strategy is a common way of dealing with the everyday demands of news production, which often do not allow verification of sources' claims, either due to lack of time, or because politicians or the public put pressure on journalists and accuse them of bias when they attempt to discredit truth-claims, or because some truth-claims are just not possible to verify. As I will discuss below, this strategy also determined how reporters interpreted the impartiality requirement in the coverage of the referendum. I will argue that the constant juxtaposition of claim and counter-claim in a binary referendum promoted a framing of the event as a competition between opponents, namely as a strategic game.

Both BBC Scotland and STV are bound by public service requirements, which include a commitment to impartiality in all their coverage. This is a central obligation set out in the Ofcom Broadcasting Code (Ofcom, 2013), as well as in the BBC's Guidelines (www.bbc.co.uk/editorialguidelines/). Traditionally impartiality has been understood as balance between opposing political views. This translates into presenting a view from one side of the argument, followed by a rebuttal from the opposing side, where each side is given the same amount of air-time over the broader course of the coverage of the campaign or issue (Norris and Sanders, 1998). In recent years the meaning of impartiality was revisited by the BBC following the publication of the 2007 Bridcut report, which proposed that the digital age requires a new approach to impartiality, namely one that involves presenting a diverse range of different opinions and not just opposing claims and counter-claims (BBC Trust, 2007).

Research carried out six years later, however, found no statistical evidence of a move from a 'seesaw' to a 'wagon wheel' view of impartiality, while party political sources continued to dominate the BBC's coverage (Wahl-Jorgensen et al., 2013). Indeed that research found a deeply ingrained paradigm in BBC reporting that still equates impartiality with seesaw balance, which according to the authors restricts the range of voices that can be heard and results in an emphasis on party political conflict (Wahl-Jorgensen et al., 2016). Although there is evidence from recent election campaigns that news values and editorial judgement are becoming increasingly important in determining how much coverage different political candidates receive (Cushion and Thomas, 2017), this does not necessarily negate the seesaw approach to balance that counteracts each claim with a counter-claim, irrespective of which source it comes from. Especially in a referendum campaign where, as opposed to elections, there are usually by default only two options, the balancing of claims and sources becomes even more straightforward for broadcasters.

A seesaw approach was thus implemented in the coverage of the 2014 referendum studied here. Most interviewees stressed that they sought balance over time, making sure that if a story or an actor from one side of the argument was more present in the coverage one evening and they were not able to counter that with a story or an actor from the other side in the same evening, then they would do this in the following days, so over time the coverage would be balanced. As one interviewee suggested:

> As I understand it, the concept of due impartiality it's not to say that you should compress down the coverage of a story because it's only favourable to one side or negative to another, but it is that you should treat that story in a fair and proportionate way and that you should give people fair and reasonable chances to respond to those stories.

The principle of allowing the other side 'reasonable chances to respond' to the claims made by their political opponents defined television's construction of impartiality, especially within a context where each official campaign followed broadcasters' coverage closely and demanded that this balance is maintained. More evidence of the seesaw approach to impartiality and fairness can be seen in how the interviewees below describe their daily reporting:

> We, so far as I know, didn't do a single report, I certainly don't think I did a single report in the course of the campaign, that didn't have both sides' views in it. And by both sides, I suppose I basically mean the Yes campaign and the No campaign. ... I think we took the view that within certainly the pieces I was doing, fairness meant in every piece allowing the other side some kind of ability to reply to the argument being put forward.

> Look, at the end of the day, we wanted to make sure that both sides in the referendum got a fair and impartial hearing and that all the regulatory and editorial standards would apply.

As explained earlier in this section, the reasons that may lead to this ritualistic approach are multiple. Pressure from the campaigns as well as the difficulty of disproving claims were both at play in the context studied here. For example, according to the interviewees below:

> Now, if we're honest, there were no hard and fast facts in the referendum campaign. Everything was a question of interpretation of the data that was presented. And with any data, you can come up with any interpretation that you think fit. The truth is we couldn't tell the answer. We could reproduce the facts, but we couldn't give them the answer that helped them decide how to vote. ... As I said, there were no hard and fast facts in the referendum, but you present the arguments and the statistics and the information as best you can and at the end of the day, people just have to make a choice.

> If I have what I regard as a fact, that I can provide indisputable, verifiable evidence to back it up, I will assert that fact as if it is the truth. If I can't,

and very often I couldn't in the referendum campaign, the nature of much of the campaign being prediction rather than history, then I would attribute what I was saying and that to me is pretty straightforward, that's how it goes, if you can prove something uncontestably and verifiably, then you say it, and if you can't, you either say you've proved it to be wrong, if you can prove it to be wrong, or you say, you point to what the evidence is, or as likely you point to who is making the claim and then try to explain the context of why they may be making that claim.

Respondents from both channels agreed that verifying what was presented as a truth claim by each side was a challenge because a lot of what was claimed concerned future developments that were hard to predict, as the second quote above suggests ('the nature of much of the campaign being prediction rather than history'), or was based on interpretation rather than fact, as the first quote proposes ('with any data, you can come up with any interpretation that you think fit'). As Tuchman observed, to deal with ambiguity reporters resort to traditional attribution and juxtaposition of claims, leaving the viewer to decide which of the two might be 'telling the truth' (1972: 665) or in this case whose predictions sounded more convincing. Another reason that imposed this approach was pressure from the campaigns:

> The difficulty with the referendum campaign is quite often there weren't definitive answers, there were only competing arguments. And that is a particular challenge, that was a particular challenge and, you know, the Yes side wanted you to declare that their argument was right, and the No side wanted you to say, no, no, surely, you can see that our argument is right. But of course much of it was argument and you can't, as an impartial broadcaster, in a referendum campaign call it one way or the other.

As seen in chapter 3, both campaigns invested in media relations and made a great effort to get their messages across, especially through television, which they both saw as neutral ground and a potentially good channel for their frames. Broadcasters were thus constantly under pressure to validate each side's position, as the interviewee above suggests ('the Yes side wanted you to declare that their argument was right, and the No side wanted you to say, no, no, surely, you can see that our argument is right'). At the same time they were also under constant scrutiny from the public, and indeed they faced intense criticism during the referendum period with protests organised by Yes supporters outside the Glasgow headquarters of BBC Scotland accusing the organisation of failing to maintain impartiality and of being biased against the pro-independence argument (Riley-Smith, 2014). Claims of bias were not based on the amount of time or opportunities offered to the two sides to express their views, but on different criteria such as the structuring of news reports or the questioning of key actors, but these were contested by BBC Scotland (*The Courier*, 2015).

These more publicly visible accusations seemed to come mainly from pro-independence supporters (members of the public and not the official Yes Scotland campaign). However, the interviews I carried out with the political communicators working for the two sides in fact revealed more frustration with broadcasters' perceived levels of impartiality coming from communicators working for parts of the No argument, some of whom felt that BBC Scotland promoted a Yes outcome and treated the No side unfairly. It is not within the scope of this research to assess either set of bias claims, nor to prove or disprove broadcasters' impartiality. What is significant about the context just described in terms of the framing of the referendum is that broadcasters were under intense pressure and their performance was being closely monitored. This made them adhere more closely to traditional claim–counter-claim rituals so as to defend themselves.

This defence strategy, however, which involved constant juxtaposition of what the two sides had to say, contributed to a focus on the competition or *game* between two opponents, which is one of the central features of the *strategic game* frame (Cappella and Jamieson, 1997). If everything said to promote one side of the debate is countered with a contrasting argument from the other side, this results in a view of the debate as one between political opponents. It has also been proposed that the *game* frame, and particularly its elements that put emphasis on journalistic analysis of opponents' strategic moves, is a defence mechanism in an environment where journalists are constantly targeted by political spin (Aalberg *et al.*, 2012). This kind of environment seems to be implied in the last quote presented above, suggesting that the two campaigns were trying to get the media 'to declare that their argument was right'.

The binary nature of the referendum itself was also highlighted by some of the journalists interviewed as a contributing factor that made the *game* frame more prominent. As the two interviewees below suggest it was more difficult to present a 'wagon wheel' of opinion with many different points of view in a referendum that had only two options on the ballot:

There were no options other than Yes and No. ... If there had been another option in the paper ... you would have had a broader range of views. But you ended up at either end of an extreme.

That probably also meant that it was harder for the different interpretations of what either an independent Scotland or a Scotland within the UK should be like to get into these reports – they probably found it harder to find their way in because we were so much trying to be fair and to split everything equally and divide it down the middle.

The *strategic game* frame, as seen in chapter 1, was developed in the study of election campaigns, where there are multiple candidates and more than two options to choose between. Still in many occasions (for instance in American elections where much of the early research on this frame is located) elections can also be binary choices between the two largest parties. Although competition and horserace is certainly not a feature limited to binary campaigns, it may be that binary debates make it more prominent.

As seen in this section, professional understandings of impartiality as balance and equivalence promoted the *strategic game* frame in the television coverage. Similar professional routines have also been associated with the conflict frame (Bartholomé *et al.*, 2015), which although conceptually distinct (Pedersen, 2014), appears to bear similarities with the *game* frame in how it emerges in the news.

Where box office meets politics: the influence of viewing figures

In addition to the balance 'ritual', another aspect contributing to the prominence of the *game* frame was a perception among interviewees, particularly from the commercial channel, that the *game* frame attracts audiences. This factor is located at the organisational level of the model of influences on journalistic content (Shoemaker and Reese, 2014).

Although, as seen in chapter 4, the *strategic game* frame was the most prominent frame in the television coverage of the referendum in the final month, and the second most prominent at other times, no interviewee spontaneously mentioned competition between political opponents when they were asked what the referendum was about. When prompted explicitly about it, some reporters appeared defensive and suggested a negative view of the *game* frame. The BBC respondent below, for example, seems to suggest that there is a conflict between 'process' and 'policy', with the latter being a 'better' focus for coverage:

> I think we always have too much focus on process ... I mean the media in the United Kingdom and Scotland generally has for years focused too much on process. ... Probably it would be better if we focused more on policy and I think in the referendum campaign, you know, arguably we could have ... did we overall talk too much about process?

This perspective perhaps reflects the negative perceptions of the *game* frame discussed in chapter 1. As explained in that chapter, political deliberation in most models of democracy is seen as a rational practice of evaluating arguments on issues of common concern. Whether one adopts a liberal or a participatory view of the democratic process, media focus on policy is more conducive to reasoned deliberation and evaluation of possible solutions than a focus on political actors' strategies to win the competition. Consistent with this interpretation, the interviewee above discusses political process and competition as a regrettable feature of UK and Scottish media.

Other interviewees though took a more matter-of-fact and less critical approach to the *game* frame. They saw the game of the campaign as part of what the referendum was and, as suggested in an earlier section of this chapter, if their role was to 'reflect' the debate, they had to reflect this aspect as well:

> Well, it was about winning. You know, you're in politics to win. You don't want to come second, you want to come up with the best answer, you want to win. So effectively, it is a horserace because it's about making sure that you have enough votes and you get your vote out.

> I wouldn't be surprised that there would be commentary of that sort because that's part of any political campaign, to offer some kind of insight and analysis of what the respective campaigns are trying to do, how they're trying to do it, and what the opinion polling is saying, for instance. So that doesn't surprise me – it would surprise me if that was all the coverage in the final month.

These respondents do not see the *game* frame as a journalistic construct, and distance themselves from it by suggesting that this was just an element of what was happening on the ground ('it was about winning', 'that's part of any political campaign'). By contrast to the interviewee quoted earlier in this section, they do not assign negative associations to the *game* frame, nor do they attribute it to the media, but they present it as a feature of the campaign itself. At other points in the interviews though, respondents, particularly from STV, the commercial broadcaster, suggested that programmes which prominently featured the *game* frame attracted large audiences. For example:

> The viewing figures were very healthy, so that's one good sign. And very often when we were covering the referendum and covering political stories, the viewing figures were particularly strong. ... We had a series of head-to-head debates and we would bring Nicola Sturgeon [at the time SNP deputy leader] to counter opponents from the other side and there were two which certainly in a political world played quite big: the clashes she had with Michael Moore [Liberal Democrat Scottish Secretary 2010–13] and

Alistair Carmichael [Liberal Democrat Scottish Secretary 2013–15]. And they had real impact in the political world. They got big viewing figures but they also had a big impact in the political world and they were commented upon quite widely. ... Our first debate with Alistair Darling [chairman of Better Together] and Alex Salmond [then SNP leader and Scottish First Minister] attracted a record audience for a political debate in Scotland – it was the sort of audience you would expect for a football match.

The excerpt above refers to one of the official leaders' debates staged by the television channels in August 2014 (there was one on BBC Scotland and one on STV, both between Alistair Darling and Alex Salmond), where senior political leaders representing the two sides presented their case and took questions from the audience, but also to an earlier debate between SNP and Liberal Democrat politicians, which took place at STV's studios. These debates and their subsequent analysis by commentators were key examples of items in the coverage that focused on political performance and competition. The interviewee here reflects the view that the *game* frame is attractive for audiences (Iyengar *et al.*, 2004) and additionally suggests that media organisations are conscious of this appeal ('they got big viewing figures', 'the sort of audience you would expect for a football match').

Televised leaders' debates provide an excellent illustration of the *strategic game* frame, as they tend to follow a rather standardised format and fulfil most of the criteria of the frame. They are competitions between political opponents with one of them eventually declared victor, while audiences are asked to decide who has won through polls (Baker and Norpoth, 1981). They are seen as focusing viewers' attention on candidate style, personality and strategy rather on than their policy proposals (Shephard and Johns, 2013), and as such they are seen as consistent with a political culture, which prioritises the performance and perception of party leaders (Coleman, 1998).

As the interviewee above suggests, the official leaders' debates on both channels indeed attracted large audiences, which reached almost a million viewers (Plunkett, 2014). Whether these figures were a result of the emphasis on competition and performance, which was central in the programmes' narrative, or whether viewers just saw them as an opportunity to hear both sides' arguments in a condensed format would require more research to establish. Perhaps viewers' reasons for watching them do not even matter in this case: the viewing figures they received were enough indication to the broadcasters that the format works. As the interviewee above suggests, 'the viewing figures were very healthy, so that's one good sign'. Moreover, the extent to which these debates were picked up and analysed by other media also added to broadcasters' perception of their importance as central events in the referendum debate:

> For the week after our debate in Glasgow between Salmond and Darling, every media outlet was full of our debate, the consequences, what happened, so, our programming did become part of the story of the campaign, and in a sense we met that objective of being in the heart of the campaign, because the campaign lived through our coverage.

As discussed earlier in this chapter and in chapter 1, the argument that the *game* frame attracts audiences is not new, but the interview data presented here additionally suggest that another perceived 'benefit' of game-framed coverage for broadcasters was that it also attracts other media's attention to something they had staged. In this way their coverage became a topic of debate in the public sphere (or 'part of the story of the campaign', as the interviewee above puts it) and generated more game-framed coverage on other platforms. As the interviewee suggests, the analysis of these debates on other media focused on their consequences for the two sides' potential to win the referendum, the performance of their leaders and what it would mean for the outcome of the vote. For the broadcasters who staged the debates, this was evidence that they had 'met that objective of being in the heart of the campaign' and therefore that they had made a contribution to public debate.

This suggests that what broadcasters think engages viewers, an organisational factor of influence (Shoemaker and Reese, 2014), promoted the *game* frame in the television coverage. In addition to that, broadcasters' perceptions of what would engage the interest of other parts of the public sphere (e.g. other media, political commentators, etc.) and make a significant impact on the course of the campaign was also significant.

If the *policy* frame was favoured by a situation where political sources had a lot of power in determining the coverage and where journalists saw their own role as presenting audiences with available options to choose between, the *game* frame was favoured by a professional understanding of objectivity as balance, and by broadcasting organisations' awareness of the appeal of game-framed news not only for audiences but also for other media. These factors contributed to legitimising it as a contribution to public debate.

Covering it like an election: the influence of previous organisational experience

A final factor impacting on the framing of the referendum as *strategic game* concerned news organisations' previous experience of covering election campaigns. All interviewees had long experience in reporting day-to-day politics in Scotland and the UK and, although both television channels had also covered the 1997 devolution referendum, journalists had considerably more experience in covering electoral contests. Reporting patterns were thus similar to what they would be during an election campaign. The *strategic game* frame is a prominent feature of most election campaigns and most studies of this frame focus on the coverage of elections, rather than on any other kind of political event. Therefore, I suggest in this section that by covering the referendum in the same way they would an election, journalists also transferred game-framed coverage to the referendum campaign.

The perceived similarities between referendum and election campaigns are reflected at the organisational level of Shoemaker and Reese's (2014) model in the fact that the same editorial guidelines apply in both types of event. Both the Ofcom code and the BBC editorial guidelines cover elections and referendums under one section and do not make major distinctions between them, other than distinctions relating to the number of political sides involved (Ofcom, 2013; www.bbc.co.uk/editorialguidelines/). This arguably encourages reporters to think of these two types of event in a similar way.

Interviewees were asked about the differences between the 2014 referendum and election campaigns, both in terms of the main features of these events, and in terms of how they worked to cover them. A number of differences were mentioned in interviewees' responses, such as the fact that the referendum was only between two competing sides while elections have multiple contenders, each side in the referendum was made up of different parties which affected how broadcasters had to distribute airtime between them, the campaign was longer than any electoral campaign, ordinary people were much more interested in the debate than they usually are in elections, every vote counted equally, the outcome would last longer and voters would not be given another chance to decide, and thus more was at stake in the referendum than during an election. For example:

> It was much longer, it comes to two and a half years. And there have been precious few referenda in Britain. You needed to recognise and remind yourself that you weren't reflecting a party political campaign. The campaign was based on a Yes or a No vote, and that cut across parties. You needed to always reflect a balance suited to the campaign, not just the political parties. So things like that you needed to do differently.

> I think the difference between the referendum and an election is that it was a binary decision. So there's two sides. … And I think the other thing that was different, as I said, from a broadcasting point of view, was the length of the campaign. And what was interesting about that was to watch over

that period how interest in it grew. Sometimes you find in election campaigns, and I've covered many election campaigns, that levels of engagement are almost, sometimes the level of engagement in the population can
drop, or at least can level out.

The interviewees above point out that the binary nature of the decision called for a different kind of 'balance suited to the campaign', not
between the different parties that usually compete in an election but
between the arguments of the Yes and No campaigns. Nonetheless neither the respondents above, nor any of the other broadcasters interviewed, suggested that there was any difference between the referendum
and elections in the competition between political sides (in fact some
interviewees suggested the referendum involved even more intensive
competition than most elections). Therefore the referendum was covered similarly to an election in terms of the extent to which broadcasters
focused on the strategies of the contestants to win the race, the performance of leading political figures, and the way their strategic moves
impacted opinion polls. Previous experience of covering elections and
the similarities between elections and referendums in regulatory terms
meant that the two events were dealt with similarly, and thus the *strategic game* frame was prominent in the referendum coverage, like it usually is in elections.

Conclusion: frame-building factors in journalistic constructions of the referendum

As explained in chapter 1, Scheufele (1999) introduced the concept of
frame-building by the media, as one component of the circular process
of framing from collective to individual level and vice versa. The media,
he suggested, construct or reproduce frames influenced by factors internal and external to news organisations, such as 'social norms and values,
organizational pressures and constraints, pressures of interest groups,
journalistic routines, and ideological or political orientations of journalists' (Scheufele, 1999: 109). According to Boesman *et al.* (2015: 2)
frame-building research should aim 'to investigate how journalistic routines and the interaction with external actors (as sources) lead to the
construction of culturally rooted frames'.

This combination between journalistic routines (such as the balance
ritual discussed in this chapter), but also journalists' own role perceptions, their previous reporting experiences of elections, organisational
understandings of what type of coverage constitutes a contribution
to the public sphere and attracts audiences, and their interaction with

external sources, was also key to the framing of the 2014 Scottish referendum examined here.

Previous studies stressed the major role political campaigns play in shaping the most prominent frames in the media during referendums (Gerth and Siegert, 2012; Hanggli, 2012). The present study confirmed this in the context of the Scottish referendum, but it also went further to explain that the reasons for the influence these sources enjoy are not always based on their elite status alone. Clearly the status assigned to the two official campaigns as the key representatives of each side of the argument was significant in ensuring their frames had broadcasters' regular attention, but in addition to that, broadcasters' own understanding of what their role was in the coverage of the campaign influenced a kind of reporting that aimed to 'mirror' and 'explain' the way the two sides defined what the referendum was about. This factor of professional role perception is arguably even more significant in determining frame-sending journalism: a non-interventionist role perception will most likely lead reporters to 'reflect' the frames of their sources, in an effort to 'explain' to audiences what is happening in the political sphere.

On the other hand, the balance ritual of seesaw reporting as a mechanism for defending journalists against accusations of bias (which were at times both public and intense during this campaign) may be a well-established journalistic convention (Tuchman, 1972), but it also has the effect of constantly juxtaposing the opposing sides in every story and presenting them as opponents, contestants in a race. This type of reporting may not necessarily promote 'objective' journalism, but it does promote a construction of politics as competition, in other words it promotes *game*-framed news coverage. Broadcasters contributed their own framing to the referendum debate by doing this, but this was not a conscious frame-setting decision on their part.

In contrast to the prevalent view that frame-setting is about journalists promoting their own preferred frames (Brüggemann, 2014), frame-setting appears to not always be a matter of preference but it also depends on pragmatic conventions. Clearly the journalists interviewed did not think they were setting a frame when they contrasted opponent views in each referendum story, and none of them said spontaneously that their personal understanding of the event was that it was a competition. The *game* frame emerged from a combination of the journalistic convention of balance, the binary nature of the campaign itself, and the fact that journalists and their organisations had similar processes for reporting a referendum as they usually do in election campaigns.

That said, journalists were not entirely oblivious to the fact that they did represent the campaign as a game between opponents. In fact, the commercial broadcaster seemed particularly conscious of the appeal this frame had not only for audiences, but also for other media. *Game*-framed coverage that focuses on political competition attracts attention both among viewers and commentators, and generates even more game-framed coverage, as commentators further analyse the performance of politicians on televised 'races'. For the commercial broadcaster, this constituted a contribution that broadcasters made to the public sphere. Thus by using the *game* frame to construct the campaign, 'journalists promote those frames that fit well with the professional criteria for journalistic selection and interpretation' (Brüggemann, 2014: 77).

The perceived attractiveness of the frame for audiences and the journalistic norm of balance were also found to be associated with the use of the conflict frame in interviews with Dutch journalists (Bartholomé *et al.*, 2015). The *strategic game* frame does not necessarily entail conflict (Pedersen, 2014), however both frames involve juxtaposition of opposing sources (competitions/games and conflicts both take place between opponents) and it is likely that for this reason both frames are associated with these factors.

The present study makes a contribution to our understanding of the *strategic game* and *policy* (issue) frames by detailing how specific influencing factors relating to journalists, their professional values, their organisations and their relationships with their political sources may combine with each other to promote these two frames. In other words it argues that there is not a single reason that these frames become prominent in the news but rather a combination of factors give rise to them.

Finally, it is important to note that both the *policy* and the *strategic game* frames were already 'culturally rooted' (Boesman *et al.*, 2015) before the referendum debate started. The former, as explained in chapter 2, was important in the relationship between Scotland and the UK throughout the history of the British union, and particularly in the second half of the twentieth century. The proposal that the 2014 referendum was a decision on a range of policy areas was certainly not new, and policy had been at the centre of the constitutional debate for decades. It was therefore a potentially resonant frame that made sense as part of this debate, perhaps even more so than the symbolic frames that the two sides also promoted, but which did not engage media attention to the same extent as policy did.

The *strategic game* frame was also culturally resonant. As explained in chapter 1, it is one of the most commonly identified frames in election campaigns around the world, and even more so in liberal democratic media systems, like the UK's. The close association of this frame with electoral contests made it a salient choice for a referendum campaign that was in many ways structured like an election, with each side of the argument represented by a group of elite political parties. Even the fact that two televised leaders' debates (a genre of coverage that is most closely associated with electoral contests) were officially organised at the end of the referendum campaign suggests that the campaign did bear similarities to an election and the transfer of the *game* frame to its coverage is not surprising.

In general broadcasters and the print media both refrained from setting their own frames in the coverage of the campaign. The next chapter will argue that this is a common feature in the coverage of several referendum campaigns in different national contexts. It will propose that referendums are constructed similarly between different national contexts and this is due to similar dynamics at play that characterise referendum campaigns more broadly as a type of political event.

6

Framing referendum campaigns in the media: towards a frame-building model

This chapter proposes a new model to analyse journalistic frame-building in the context of highly contested referendum campaigns, based on the insights generated in previous chapters. This model systematises the aspects proposed in the previous chapter as encouraging the reproduction of frames promoted by political sources and their reframing through the *strategic game* frame. It also combines these findings with what we know from previous research on other referendums in different national contexts. As I will argue below, the model proposed here can potentially help explain frame-building in referendums more broadly in liberal/democratic corporatist media systems.

The model, which is presented in figure 3, consists of two sets of elements. I propose that the first set (factors 1–4) creates an environment that encourages journalists to reproduce the frames promoted by political campaigns. The second set (factors 5–9) fosters the 'reframing' of these frames in the coverage through the use of the *strategic game* frame. In this chapter I will explain each element of the model, drawing on the findings of the present and previous empirical studies.

The proposed model aims to provide a useful basis to be tested in future research on new referendum cases in liberal/democratic corporatist media systems. It makes an analytical contribution to our understanding of how media frames are shaped during highly contested political campaigns and it sets new avenues to be further explored and expanded in research on the mediation of referendums.

Clearly there are substantial differences between referendums in different parts of the world, especially between democratic and non-democratic countries (Qvortrup, 2014: 248), and broad generalisations across diverse nations are risky. However in many Western democracies referendums share some common principles (Butler and Ramney, 1994; Qvortrup, 2014). Particularly, as will be discussed in this chapter, findings from framing studies conducted so far on the media coverage of referendums in liberal (Scotland, Quebec) and democratic corporatist

(Denmark, Switzerland) media systems reveal similarities which may be connected to key features these media systems share, as identified by Hallin and Mancini (2004).

Despite their distinctive individual circumstances, the above referendum framing studies came to similar conclusions regarding how referendums were framed by the media in the countries they each studied. This suggests that there may be some common features in the ways the media work when covering referendum campaigns which transcend national contexts. By highlighting these aspects and organising them in the form of a frame-building model (figure 3), I aim to address the call made by Aalberg *et al.* (2012: 173) for a more comprehensive investigation of the contextual conditions that might give rise to the *strategic game* frame (and also to the reproduction of political sources' advocacy frames) in the news, by focusing particularly here on referendums as a particular type of political event.

This chapter will argue that, according to existing research, the factors which are proposed in this frame-building model as potentially playing a role in journalists' reproduction of their sources' frames and their employment of the *strategic game* frame are common in Western democracies and are especially shared among certain journalistic cultures. Based on these similarities, the proposed framework provides an explorative account of how the media frame referendums in these media systems.

Apart from the cautioning that, as mentioned above, cross-national generalisations are risky by default, the idea that complex national contexts and their particularities can be reduced to broad classifications is also potentially problematic. Thus the model proposed in this chapter should be read as an initial proposal to be tested, qualified and expanded with further case studies in the same and in other countries with liberal and corporatist media systems. Before presenting this framework, though, I will briefly review what previous research tells us about the framing of campaigns as *strategic game* and *issue (policy)* in electoral contexts, which is the type of political event where they are primarily encountered and theorised.

Election frame-building

The use of the same media frames to discuss elections and referendums invites audiences to think of them along similar lines. Indeed, both events involve a high degree of political competition, and the *strategic game* frame lends itself particularly well to telling the story in the news. It satisfies news values such as drama, conflict, personalisation and references to elite politicians (Aalberg *et al.*, 2012). It allows journalists to tie

together originally unrelated elements, such as opinion polls, party publications and political interviews, into a coherent storyline (Robinson,
1998: 105). It also allows them to maintain a critical distance from all
their sources, appearing not to be taking anyone's side, while at the same
time providing 'expert' analysis, without attempting to prove or disprove
the substance of what sources claim.

Lawrence (2000: 96) argues that the *game* frame is so common
in election coverage that it forms a 'master narrative' reminiscent of
sports coverage, whereby 'election day is the goal line, and everything
that happens during the campaign is significant only as it pertains to
a politician's (or a party's) chances of getting across the line'. In this
context, she suggests, policy debates are relevant as a field where political opponents clash and compete with each other in their effort to
win, therefore policy debates are most relevant when they are likely
to have a clear outcome of victory for one of the opponents. As decision time approaches in the form of the day of voting, the *game* frame
becomes more prominent in the news, especially when contest between
elites is close. In another study Dunaway and Lawrence (2015) find
that although this journalistic frame is broadly more common in commercial than public service media (a finding corroborated by several
other studies, for instance Dimitrova and Strömbäck, 2011), when an
election race is close, all types of media converge on a game-framed
narrative.

The tendency to *game*-frame electoral coverage is seen as a development of the past three or four decades when a shift is said to have taken
place in journalism from focusing on political candidates' proposals and
speeches to their performance, motives and tactics (Patterson, 1993).
This is part of a broader argument that sees mainstream media coverage
of politics as deteriorating, prioritising entertainment over serious news
coverage, producing cynical and populist coverage of politics, focusing
on spin and scandal and thus diluting the democratic importance of the
fourth estate (Sparks, 1991; Blumler and Gurevitch, 1995). This argument sees journalists as responsible for creating poorly informed voters
with a distrust for the political system. This later point, as was seen
in chapter 1, is also central in much thinking around the *game* frame
(Cappella and Jamieson, 1997).

This shift in the content of journalism is often seen as connected to
changes in the way politics is done, which took place during the same
period (political communication campaigns themselves have become
more professionalised and personalised) but also to the increased commercial and production pressures affecting the news industry. These
are global phenomena affecting most Western countries. Despite some

differences between countries with different media systems in the extent to which the frame is used during elections (for example less commercialised media with more state regulation in less binary political systems are said not to have as much game-framed coverage – see Binderkrantz and Green-Pedersen, 2009), the *strategic game* frame is highly present across many different countries, media and electoral contexts.

The transferal of the *strategic game* frame from elections to referendum campaigns is therefore often seen as a natural step in the literature. De Vreese and Semetko (2002) found that in different media's coverage of the 2000 Danish referendum on the adoption of the euro, between 25 and 69 per cent of the media were dominated by the 'strategy' frame. This mostly involved using war, game and sport metaphors. Similarly, Robinson (1998: 88) argues that the 1980 Quebec independence referendum was treated by the media as an election campaign invoking 'a pre-existing sports style of narration based on adversarialism', which is normally associated with election coverage. She suggests that in that referendum, the *game* frame legitimated confrontation between the two opposing sides, in an attempt to simplify the mediated narrative of the event and make it more engaging for audiences. At the same time though, it directed people's attention away from the commonalities the Yes and No campaigns may have had or from those aspects of the referendum that involve citizens engaging in deliberation about their collective future.

Another strand of media framing studies of referendums and citizen consultations (Gerth and Siegert, 2012; Hanggli, 2012; Atickan, 2015) focuses on issue-specific advocacy frames rather than on generic frames like the *policy* and *strategic game* frames. Although some of these studies (Gerth and Siegert, 2012) do identify a minor presence of 'contest' frames in the coverage ('contest' is a frame which, as noted in chapter 1, can be associated but does not coincide with the *game* frame), their focus is more on whether advocacy arguments, promoted by political campaigns, are adopted or rejected by the media and/or public opinion. These studies conclude that, in the different cases they analysed, the media adopted political sources' frames and did not create their own – a finding that is also shared by the present study. As was seen in chapters 3, 4 and 5, Scottish media reproduced primarily the *policy* frame, which was promoted by both campaigns, as well as – to a lesser extent – a set of symbolic frames that they also took from the official campaigns. They did not, however, create original substantive frames of their own, with the exception of the *democratic achievement* and *national division* frames, which had very marginal presence in all the media, as was seen in chapter 4.

The studies reviewed above are mainly located in Western liberal (Scotland, Canada) and democratic corporatist (Switzerland, Denmark) media systems (Hallin and Mancini, 2004). According to Hallin and Mancini's (2004) theory of media systems, Western countries may be split in three ideal type categories, with different features relating to the relationship between media and politics, the degree of professionalisation of journalism, the characteristics of the press, and the intervention of the state in the media. These three types of media systems are the liberal model, the democratic corporatist model and the polarised-pluralist model.

Hallin and Mancini (2004) acknowledge the inherent problems in grouping together and making generalisations about diverse national contexts, which are in many ways different from each other, but as a general guiding classification their model has been useful in analytical accounts of the role of the media in politics in different countries. The same disclaimer also holds for the frame-building model proposed in this chapter, whose discussion draws on both Hallin and Mancini's classification and a small number of referendum framing studies in different national contexts reviewed above (including the Scottish case): the model put forward in this chapter is meant as a broad classification for analytical purposes, rather than as a generalising clustering of countries that have some similarities (but also differences) to each other. This proposal can be tested and refined in different cases, rather than be read as a definitive universal account. Despite this, the proposed model makes an important analytical contribution to our understanding of how media frames are shaped during highly contested political campaigns by combining and systematising findings from this and from previous studies, and by proposing relationships to be further explored in future research. The model proposed here is meant as an account that links media system characteristics to frame-building in referendums for analytical purposes, and it is not meant to imply that the countries mentioned in the discussion are identical.

With this disclaimer in mind, the next section will explore a network of conditions in liberal and democratic corporatist media systems, whose combination may contribute to a rather homogeneous media construction of referendums, based on the present and on previous research. These are the component elements of the analytical model presented in figure 3.

Frame-building factors

Chapter 5 argued that the high *dependence of journalists on political campaigns as news sources* (1) and their own *non-interventionist journalistic role perceptions* (2) encouraged journalists to reproduce the frames promoted by the two sides of the referendum campaign. These two factors are thus connected to 'frame sending', namely to the reproduction of elite source frames (Brüggemann, 2014), in my proposed frame-building model (figure 3). In the next paragraphs I will argue that these two factors – (1) and (2) – are common in both liberal and democratic corporatist media systems and may therefore apply to media framing of referendums across these national contexts.

Both the degree of influence politicians enjoy on the media and the extent to which journalists are (or see themselves as being) interventionist in the ideology of the content they produce are closely connected with national journalistic cultures in different media systems (van Dalen *et al.*, 2012).

As Hanitzsch and Vos (2016) point out, journalistic roles are discursive constructions, rather than reflections, of what journalism is and how it functions in society. This means that they reflect how journalists talk and think about what they do, which does ultimately have an impact on how they perform their work, but represents rather an ideal notion of how journalists see their performance. Their research found that the 'Western' model of journalism, which prioritises journalistic autonomy from politics and non-interventionism, operates across different Western media systems and makes journalists' perceptions of their role more similar across countries. As Hanitzsch *et al.* (2011: 273) suggest, 'Western journalists are generally less supportive of any active promotion of particular values or ideas[1] … Journalists from non-western contexts, on the other hand, tend to be more interventionist'.

Although different national media systems are still relevant in shaping journalistic cultures and role perceptions, there appears to be a tendency for homogenisation of journalists' role perceptions in the West and particularly among North European cultures. Van Dalen *et al.* (2012) found, for example, that North European journalists from both liberal (UK) and corporatist media systems (Denmark, Germany) share similar non-interventionist values and differ from their colleagues in Spain (a polarised pluralist media system) who see their role as sacerdotal towards politics rather than pragmatic, and partisan rather than impartial. Journalists in Northern European countries were not found to be as different from each other in these respects.

As well as adopting non-interventionist roles, journalists in Western/ Northern European countries tend to perceive themselves as distant from political and economic centres of power and they don't see political influence as significant in their work, as opposed to journalists from non-Western countries (Hanitzsch and Mellado, 2011; Hanitzsch *et al.*, 2011). This though does not mean that political elites are not influential in shaping media content in the West, but rather that their impact is not perceived as important by journalists. Indeed political elites were identified as crucial in framing referendum debates in Switzerland (Hanggli and Kriesi, 2010; Gerth and Siegert, 2012), as well as in the Scottish case study analysed in this book. Although in these contexts political actors do not explicitly impose their perspectives on journalistic content, they remain the central, most newsworthy sources for journalists in political coverage and enjoy an indirect but still highly privileged role in defining public issues.

In liberal media systems (such as the UK's or Canada's), journalism is typically independent of the political system and is governed mainly by commercial criteria and a critical distance from politicians, with the exception of the press in the UK, which as mentioned previously is openly partisan and has explicit agendas and political alliances, which were particularly emphatic in both the 2014 and the subsequent 2016 EU referendum. These features of the press make the British media a less characteristic example of the liberal model (Schudson, 2001: 167). That said, both print and broadcast journalists in liberal systems have traditionally relied heavily on official political sources for news content (Hallin and Mancini, 2004). This means that the media remain close to the political system, even when they are editorially independent from it. The same holds for the democratic corporatist systems of mainland European countries (such as Denmark or Switzerland). These are characterised by a tradition of ideologically oriented press, which is becoming increasingly depoliticised and commercial, and an independent broadcasting system modelled upon the BBC.

Journalists appear to refrain from introducing new ways of understanding issues, but instead replicate the frames of their sources during highly contested referendum campaigns in both the above types of media systems. These source frames are usually advocacy frames promoting the interests of each side. In the case of the Scottish referendum advocacy frames mainly consisted in issue (*policy*) frames, whereas in other cases in other countries these were issue-specific frames (Hanggli and Kriesi, 2010; Gerth and Siegert, 2012; Hanggli, 2012; Atickan, 2015). Thus a common finding between studies in both liberal and democratic corporatist media systems is that journalists do not interfere with the framing of a referendum campaign and let political sources be the primary definers. The only option for them to contribute to the construction of the event is through the introduction of the *strategic game* frame, as will be explained later in this chapter.

Based on the above discussion, I therefore propose that journalists' *non-interventionist role perceptions* (1) in these media systems and *their high dependence on political actors as sources* (2), can restrict journalistic frame-setting (namely the extent to which journalists create and shape frames – Brüggemann, 2014), during referendum campaigns. This in turn gives the opportunity to political actors to shape media frames.

Indeed journalistic roles have also been seen by others as potential influences in frame building: more specifically, van Dalen *et al.* (2012) tested a connection between a pragmatic journalistic role perception and the use of the *game* frame in different countries, but although they found support for this connection in some countries (Spain), they did not in others (Denmark, UK). The findings from the qualitative interviews presented in the previous chapter of this book indicate that another connection that is worth testing in bigger quantitative studies in different contexts is the one between interventionism, the centrality of political sources in daily journalistic routines, and journalistic frame-setting.

As for which particular political sources' frames become more used in the media, it has been previously proposed (Hanggli, 2012) that *powerful organisations and prominent political figures* become the main frame-builders of a referendum (3), especially when they repeat their messages to the media very frequently, but in addition to this the present study has also argued that powerful sources' frames are more likely to be adopted by the media when they are contested by *both* sides of the argument.

For example, in the Scottish case, the *constitutional change* and *self-determination* frames were promoted by the No and Yes sides respectively and they were prominent both in their advertising and media relations messages. The latter was one of the key messages of the Yes campaign, repeated in most advertisements and speeches by the campaign's main figureheads in the form of the slogan 'Scotland's future in Scotland's hands'. Despite the fact that it was promoted regularly by powerful political figures, the frame did not become the most prominent frame in the media. Even in the *Sunday Herald*, the only outlet that supported a Yes outcome, *self-determination* appeared in only 10 per cent of the coverage sampled. This suggests that power and prominence of the political sources promoting a frame and a lot of repetition of the frame are not always enough.

However, source *frames where both sides present their contrasting claims* (4) during a referendum campaign offer more scope for debate and conflict, and are therefore more newsworthy. As argued in chapter 3, the *policy* frame was proactively and strategically promoted by the Yes and No sides and thus it became one of the most dominant frames in the media. Moreover, as argued in the same chapter, that frame was consistent with long-standing discourses around Scotland's relationship with the UK and was thus 'culturally resonant' (Snow and Benford, 1988).

So far it has been argued that the four factors presented above (1–4) work together to form an environment that is conducive to frame-sending political actors' frames (figure 3). However journalists do not only replicate these frames but also 'reframe' them, as was seen in chapter 5, through the *strategic game* narrative. Below I propose five further factors which may be connected to the prominence of this latter frame.

First, as seen in the previous chapter, the *binary nature* (5) of the referendum question was considered by many journalists in the Scottish case as a reason that influenced media framing in oppositional terms. The limitation of the debate to only two options acts against reporting a more diverse spectrum of opinion and encourages a competitive construction of the two campaign sides. Other referendums where the choice was binary also saw a heavy reliance on the *game* frame (e.g. de Vreese and Semetko, 2004). I therefore propose that binary campaigns are more likely to be framed as a *game* between opponents than those where more options are available.

Clearly binarism is not only a feature of referendums but also of some election campaigns, particularly in political systems where there are just two main parties. My proposition that binarism is connected with the presence of the *game* frame in the news is also supported by studies suggesting that political systems where elections are multi-party contests tend to generate less *game*-framed coverage (Binderkrantz and Green-Pedersen, 2009). Like an election with more than two major parties competing for the vote, a referendum with more than two opposing sides may attract less *game*-framed coverage.

Second, the fact that major political parties and politicians are commonly assigned (by the Electoral Commission in the Scottish case) as representing each outcome in referendums makes them by definition the key players in the coverage. This can lead to a framing of the debate as a contest between these specific political camps rather than as a broader social debate. These parties and politicians are often already in direct opposition with each other before the referendum, and represent different positions in the political spectrum. In the Scottish case, the parties that made up Yes Scotland and Better Together were long-standing opponents contesting elections for government in London and in Scotland, and the same was the case in all other referendums where media framing studies have been conducted.

When referendums are thus *conducted within the context of national party politics* (6), it is not only possible that voters' evaluations of the performance of politicians before the referendum might influence the vote (as proposes the second-order election thesis – see LeDuc, 2002; Qvortrup, 2014), but also that the referendum becomes associated with an 'electoral' competition between these pre-established political opponents. Moreover, when *media regulations and editorial standards make no substantial distinction* (7) between elections and referendums (as in broadcasting in both the Scottish and Quebec cases), other than those relating to the number of participating parties and the required split of attention between them, this may encourage a similar journalistic treatment of the referendum to that of an election. When this is the case, both the key people/parties used as sources and the rules that guide the reporting of their views are more or less the same as in an election campaign, and this might encourage journalists to treat these events similarly as a *strategic game* between political sides.

Third, *an understanding of objectivity or impartiality as balance* (8) can lead to a constant juxtaposition of the views of political opponents and thus emphasise strategic competition between them, as was argued in chapter 5. This factor is not relevant for media which are not expected to be impartial. For example the press in the UK does not have to adhere to any rules of impartiality and is indeed openly partisan. However broadcasting is obliged to adhere to some form of balanced reporting in most Western democracies (Hopmann *et al.*, 2011).

Although objectivity and impartiality are accepted as important journalistic values internationally (Hanitzsch and Mellado, 2011), how journalists interpret these values differs across cultures (Skovsgaard *et al.*, 2013). In liberal media systems (Hallin and Mancini, 2004), the objectivity norm is central and it is understood as 'neutrality and balance' in political coverage, an 'informational' style of journalism 'free' of opinion and independent of political partiality. In other words, journalistic objectivity is perceived as 'expressing fairly the position of each side in a political dispute' (Patterson, 1998).

The most common way of understanding and implementing objectivity, though, is as balance, namely giving equal access (presence) and space (airtime) to opposing political views (Hopmann *et al.*, 2011; Skovsgaard *et al.*, 2013), an understanding which, as was seen in chapter 5, is also dominant in British broadcasting. It has in fact been so dominant in this context for such a long time that Wahl-Jorgensen *et al.* (2016) speak of a deeply entrenched paradigm of 'impartiality-as-balance' in public service broadcasting.

Similarly, in democratic corporatist media systems, broadcasting is required by law to be politically and ideologically balanced, especially in its news coverage. The BBC's public service broadcasting model of 'neutral' reporting has been particularly influential on television in democratic corporatist media systems (Hallin and Mancini, 2004). This suggests a similar centrality of the balance norm.

An understanding of objectivity as meaning balance and juxtaposition of opposing views with no interference from the journalist is positively associated with non-interventionist journalistic role perceptions of the media as a 'mirror' and 'forum' for debate (Skovsgaard *et al.*, 2013), which are also dominant in the media systems discussed here. The balance norm is also a practical way for journalists to defend themselves 'from public criticism, embarrassment or lawsuits' (Schudson, 2001: 165). These risks are particularly high in referendum campaigns. Thus the balance norm becomes even more important than usual as a journalistic defence mechanism during referendums, and this may also contribute to the high prominence of the *game* frame.

Finally, journalists may be encouraged to produce *game*-framed coverage by *organisational perceptions* (9) that view the *game* of the campaign not only as newsworthy and attractive for audiences but also as a contribution to public debate. Providing a platform for politicians to compete with each other can be viewed by news organisations as appealing to audiences and as making a contribution to the public sphere (see chapter 5), which acts as a further motivation for such coverage.

Commercial considerations (as, in this case, the need to appeal to audiences) are important in both liberal and democratic corporatist media systems. In the latter, the media have had strong attachments to both politics and commercialisation in the past, but they have shifted away from the former and towards the latter more recently (Hallin and Mancini, 2004). In liberal systems too, where the dominance of market rules in the media is a central feature, even public service broadcasting is said to be 'increasingly affected by market logic' (Hallin and Mancini, 2004: 232). The *game* frame satisfies this market logic, and is thus consistent with commercial considerations in both types of media system.

The nine elements (1–9) outlined in this section create a conducive environment that may encourage journalists to (a) reproduce the frames promoted by political elites, and (b) reframe these political campaign frames by introducing the *game* frame. The interaction of these nine elements is illustrated in figure 3.

Factors identified in previous literature on the game frame, which were reviewed in chapter 1, such as the closeness of the electoral contest, the proximity to polling date, or the commercial/public service status of the media, are also influential in promoting *game*-framed news in referendum campaigns. The model proposed here does not mention these factors because it intends to highlight additional aspects relating particularly to the coverage of referendum campaigns, beyond these general triggers.

Frame-building model for referendums

Brüggemann (2014: 67) suggests that frame-building research should explore particularly under which conditions journalists pursue frame-setting (creating their own news frames) or frame-sending (reproducing the frames of their sources). The model in figure 3 contributes to thinking in this area by attempting to address this question for the context of referendum campaigns in liberal/democratic corporatist media systems. It expands on the distinction between frame-setting and frame-sending by proposing factors, which may encourage frame-sending but also 'frame reframing' through the introduction of the *strategic game* frame.

In the context of highly contested referendums, journalists are unlikely to admit to having their own personal frames and even less likely to

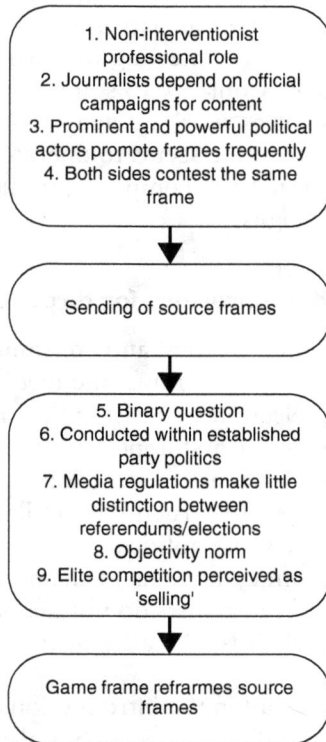

Figure 3 Frame-building in referendums

frame news coverage based on personal frames. In other words, referendum campaigns do not usually provide much fertile ground for frame-setting. Non-interventionist journalistic role perceptions and dependence on official political campaigns on a day-to-day basis seem to encourage the reproduction of political sources' frames.

In addition, when the referendum question is binary and the debate is polarised between just two options, when objectivity is interpreted as balance and equivalence, when the referendum is conducted within pre-established national party politics, and/or media organisations view political competition and politicians' performance as attracting audiences, journalists may reframe source frames using the *strategic game* frame in their coverage. This latter though does not clash with nor necessarily takes attention away from political sources' advocacy frames, but works with them.

Like other generic, journalistic frames, the *strategic game* frame is 'more apparent in playing-up, neglecting or juxtaposing advocacy frames' (de Vreese, 2012: 367). It offers cues as to how political sources' frames are to be interpreted (namely as strategic moves in politicians' efforts to win the referendum, or as part of a competition between them and their opponents) without contesting or putting under examination politicians' core proposals. Contrary to some of the literature reviewed in chapter 1, which sees it as working against substantial coverage of politics, the *strategic game* frame seems to operate more as a 'reframing' frame rather than an 'alternative', competing frame in the narrative context of referendum campaigns.

Framing, ideology and implications for direct democracy

By sending political source frames and 'reframing', or re-organising them, through the *strategic game* frame, the media essentially construct referendums similarly to elections, at least in the journalistic cultures discussed above. This may not at first appear to be an ideological decision as it is not necessarily a conscious construction. As explained previously, elections and referendums are structured similarly by legislative and regulating bodies, with the same political actors/parties contesting both. The features of referendum campaigns in themselves may thus encourage this construction, and journalists do not necessarily decide to frame them this way nor do they 'distort' reality by doing so. So why does this framing matter?

As explained in more detail in the introduction to this book, there are long-standing debates in political science, but also in mainstream political discourse, on the merits or disadvantages of having direct forms of democracy. According to Butler and Ramney, the central argument of proponents of direct democracy is that with its different instruments, including referendums, it allows:

> the full, direct, and unmediated participation of all citizens. The citizens, they declare, should set the agenda, discuss the issues and determine the policies. ... If the citizens' ideas and preferences are expressed only by squeezing them through the minds and mouths of representatives, they are bound to emerge distorted ... citizens' civic potentials can be realized only by their direct and full participation in public affairs. (Butler and Ramney, 1994: 12–13)

As this excerpt suggests, citizen participation in setting the agenda and discussing the issues without the mediation of political representatives is a key distinctive feature of direct democracy and its main advantage. According to its proponents, by participating directly in the decision-making process, citizens become more competent in public affairs and self-government. They achieve this not simply by considering politicians' arguments and turning out to vote (this is something they can also do in representative democracy anyway), but by setting the debate, deliberating the issues and fully participating in the political process. This kind of democracy is not feasible all of the time in modern societies, and this is why in most cases representative democracy is supplemented by direct democracy initiatives, such as referendums, which provide opportunities to maximise citizen participation.

However, the mediated construction of referendum campaigns which was presented earlier, and which, as discussed above, is rather common in different countries does not encourage citizens to fulfill the potential of direct democracy initiatives as envisaged by their proponents. By letting political elites set the frames of the debate, with little interference other than emphasising their political strategies, performance and competition, journalists do not put citizens at the centre of the political process of direct democracy initiatives. Indeed the framing practices they follow are more fitting for classic representative democracy, giving control and a central role to political actors, and making little distinction as to where the discursive power lies in a referendum as opposed to an election. Both journalistic non-interventionism and an understanding of impartiality as balance between formal political interests are consistent with a liberal view of the role of the media in society, which does not empower citizens to be part of their own governance.

A common problem that opponents of direct democracy highlight in relation to referendums is that they are ultimately controlled by elites, because political actors decide if and when a referendum will be held and how the question will be phrased, they are the key funders of the campaigns promoting different outcomes (Tierney, 2012) and they are thus able to strategically direct referendums to benefit their own interests (Altman, 2011). By allowing political elites to also determine the grounds on which deliberations take place in the public sphere, the media further enable this control and construct what is a relatively rare instance of direct democracy in representative terms. In these terms, referendums may be treated as just another way for political elites to confirm their positions through the stamp of approval of the public vote, 'let off political steam' from the system, and remove controversial issues from the public agenda (Qvortrup, 2014). In this way, referendums become more easily tools in the hands of politicians rather than genuine opportunities for the public to deliberate and take on a protagonist role in politics.

The media framing of referendums discussed in this chapter reproduces a liberal view of democracy as this was defined in chapter 1, whereby the representatives of the people have the first say in determining even direct democracy initiatives. In this perspective, citizens fulfil their role in politics by staying well informed on what different political elites propose and by making a decision between these proposals (Strömbäck, 2005) and the media fulfil their role by presenting citizens with the information they need to do this. As seen in chapter 5, this duty to inform about what politicians have to say is part of journalists' perception of their role in referendums as well as in elections. The media make little distinction between direct and representative forms of democracy in regards to who should have the first say in framing the debate: political elites remain the unquestioned primary definers in both cases.

Such framing may go unnoticed in the news because it is seen as 'reflecting' the way things are. As argued earlier, referendum campaigns themselves are usually organised around major political players and parties, rather than around citizen groups. However, things are the way they are because there is social consensus about them and this social consensus is also constructed and reproduced by the way the media define, select, represent, structure and shape political reality.

As Hall (1982: 60) puts it, 'a pivotal element in the production of consent [is] how things [are] defined', or framed, through language. Language does not just 'reflect' reality, but provides 'selective definitions of "the real" ... selecting and presenting, structuring and shaping' (Hall, 1982: 60). If referendums are talked about as a game between political actors, where they have the power to define what is at stake and what criteria people should apply in deciding how to vote, rather than as an opportunity for people to determine the political process, this understanding becomes normalised and accepted as the status quo, especially since most people get few opportunities to experience direct democracy in their lifetime. Choosing to frame direct democracy as a debate between politicians helps construct 'consensus' or a collective commonsense understanding, so that it might seem odd to propose that any other possibility might be conceivable. It positions citizens and journalists in a secondary role, as 'consumers' of political messages rather than as shapers of their own frames.

For these reasons the construction of referendums as *strategic game* and the reproduction of elite advocacy frames in media coverage carries ideological implications. This does not imply that the media abuse their power, mislead or manipulate the electorate as critical analyses of ideology often suggest (van Dijk, 1995: 11), but rather that they are part of the system that reproduces existing political structures. The conditions (perceptions of journalistic roles, balance norms, structure of political campaigns, and so on) that favour this construction and are part of the frame-building model presented earlier in this chapter, are also shaped by the same establishment that is reinforced through the framing process. If framing referendums is a struggle over meaning, the struggle is mainly defined as one between political actors and 'official' campaigns, who are journalists' central news sources. As van Dijk (1995) suggests, mainstream media are part of a power structure of groups and institutions whose procedures and discourses subtly and indirectly support the status quo.

Conclusion

Different studies on referendum campaigns in liberal and democratic corporatist media systems broadly agree that the media usually give high prominence to *game* and/or contest frames and replicate the frames of political elites, but do not interfere by introducing original frames of their own. This chapter argued that this is likely connected to similar dynamics at play in different referendum campaigns. The structure of a campaign itself seems to influence how it is framed in the news, as do the conditions journalists work in during it. This chapter proposed a frame-building model for referendums, which organises these factors in an analytical schema.

The chapter contextualised the findings from the analysis of the Scottish referendum case, which were presented in detail in previous chapters, within existing research on other referendum and citizen consultation campaigns in other national contexts. It has argued that these contexts share features, which are connected with the media systems they are part of and which may contribute to the similarities identified in the framing between them.

The chapter combined insights from the present and previous research in the form of a model that explains frame-building in different referendum campaigns within these media systems. It argued that referendums, as a type of political event, do not encourage journalistic frame-setting, because neither the media systems themselves nor the highly contested and polarised conditions of a referendum allow journalistic interventionism. The dependence of journalists on the official campaigns and their own occupational values both direct them towards replicating sources' frames (in a more or less partisan way, depending on whether the specific media are committed to objectivity norms or are openly politicised) and in introducing the *game* frame to reframe these advocacy frames within a narrative that is both attractive for audiences and has perceived civic value in the public sphere.

The model presented here (Figure 3) is based on a small number of case studies, and should serve as the basis for further research in these as well as in other national contexts. The model is particularly relevant in liberal and/or democratic corporatist media systems and it would be enhanced by comparative examination within these as well as other systems.

The next chapter will discuss the findings of this study in light of more recent developments following the 2016 referendum on EU membership. It will argue that the media framing of the latter was not dissimilar to that of the 2014 Scottish referendum (with the exception of Scottish broadcasting where the coverage was indeed quite different from that in England) and that similar conditions to the ones explored in this chapter appear to be connected to a similar framing in the 2016 EU referendum case. This more recent referendum, therefore, as I will argue next, provides further supporting evidence that the frame-building model presented here can indeed explain other, newer referendums.

Finally the next chapter will also discuss further avenues for framing research in a changing media environment. Although, as argued at different points in this book, 'old' mainstream media remain important in the digital age, their role is increasingly transformed by the use of online platforms in political communication. These operate in different ways from traditional, mainstream media organisations, and they allow political actors direct access to attempt to influence audiences, without the intervention of journalistic gatekeepers. The final chapter will problematise the applicability of frame-building research like the present study in this kind of context and propose new avenues that future research may explore.

Note

1 Clearly this is rather the case with broadcast journalists than with print journalists, who, as mentioned often through this chapter, are often openly partisan.

Conclusion

'The issue of decision-making' in a referendum, proposes Tierney (2012: 238), 'cannot be divorced from that of issue-framing'. Although as suggested in chapter 1 research on framing effects does not always confirm direct media impact on voting behaviour, the frames that become prominent in the media play a significant role in shaping public debate beyond individual media outlets and define the terms in which decision-making is talked about in public discourse. The aim of this book has been to provide an account of how mainstream media frames are shaped during highly contested referendum campaigns, and the previous chapter proposed an original frame-building model to do just that.

As was stated in the introduction to this book, much of what has been discussed here relates not only to referendums as a distinctive category of political event, but more broadly to the process of the journalistic mediation of politics. In fact one of the arguments that run through the chapters of this book is that journalists often treat referendums like elections, giving political actors the power to determine the main frames and representing the political process as a competition between these actors. Despite the fact that referendums and elections do have some aspects in common, this book has argued that as an instrument of direct democracy the former should be more distinct and should give a more central role to public deliberation and frame-setting by non-elite actors. By placing political representatives at the centre of a direct democratic process, journalists make it possible for them to use and manipulate referendums for their own purposes.

The frame-building model I introduced in chapter 6 expands thinking around media frame-building in referendum campaigns. It was argued in that chapter that the proposed model may account for referendums beyond the ones it was based on, because its elements are ingrained in particular media systems. In this chapter, I will explore the applicability of my model in new referendum contexts. More specifically I will suggest that the UK's 2016 referendum on EU membership appears to also fit the model well, and the same factors might be connected to similar frame-building in the mainstream media. I will then conclude the discussion with a broader consideration of the role of online platforms in altering traditional political communication processes and the directions which frame-building research will be required to take in the future to deal with this shifting environment.

Frame-building during the 2016 EU referendum

Like in the Scottish referendum, the coverage of the 2016 referendum on the UK's membership of the EU was dominated by *game* and *policy* frames. In the final month of that campaign, 65 per cent of the referendum coverage on the *BBC News at Six* daily news bulletin contained the *game* frame and 94 per cent the *policy* frame (Dekavalla, forthcoming). This trend was consistent in other mainstream media as well: according to a content analysis of print and broadcast coverage of the whole campaign by Deacon *et al.* (2016), three issues dominated the media coverage of the EU debate: the economy; immigration (both of which are *policy* areas); and the conduct of the campaign itself (one of the components of the *strategic game* frame). The same findings are also supported by Cushion and Lewis who suggest that half of the EU referendum coverage they analysed 'related to the process of the Referendum, notably ... campaign walkabouts or the strategies of competing sides, as well as public opinion towards the EU and the way people would vote' (2016: 40). Although the latter two studies did not measure explicitly the presence of the *game* frame, their criteria provide a relatively close fit with the indicators of the *strategic game* frame, as these were defined in chapters 1 and 4 of this book.

The similar framing between the Scottish and the EU referendums may be accounted for by the frame-building model proposed in chapter 6 (Figure 3 on page 141), which appears to be applicable in both referendums. Most of the factors proposed in the model also hold for the 2016 EU referendum. For instance, the 2016 EU referendum was also a *binary campaign* between *prominent and powerful members of the UK* established party political scene (factors 3, 5 and 6 in figure 3). The Conservative Party was split between Eurosceptics who led the Vote Leave campaign (with Boris Johnson a leading senior figure) and pro-EU Conservative Party members at the head of the cross-party Stronger In campaign (with then prime minister David Cameron in the lead). Labour and the Liberal Democrats were also in favour of remaining in the EU but were less visible than the Conservatives in the media. Although there was not one-to-one correspondence between political parties and the two official campaigns, and this time members of the same party competed against each other, the political actors involved in the two camps were again pre-established political opponents before the referendum, with Boris Johnson being considered at the time as a future contender who could potentially take over the leadership of the Conservative Party from Cameron. Therefore there was established competition between politicians from the two camps, while both these and other key members of the Conservative Party were very active in promoting campaign messages. In the EU referendum too, *both campaigns contested the* policy *frame* (factor 4 in figure 3). The Leave campaign focused on the impact of the referendum outcome for immigration and the Remain campaign on the economy as the key criteria people should employ to make their decision (Keaveney, 2016). Policy proposals may not have been detailed, but the political debate was nevertheless focused on what changes would result from a vote to remain or leave the EU for immigration policy and the economy.

In this campaign, like in previous referendums, the *dependence of the media on the two political campaigns* (factor 2 in figure 3) is confirmed by the fact that 'the overwhelming voices heard in the news were by Leave or Remain campaigners. More independent actors – for instance from think tanks or academics – made up a tiny share of sources used to inform coverage' (Cushion and Lewis, 2016: 40). Although no research on journalistic working practices during this campaign had been published at the time of writing, the above content analysis finding suggests a high dependence on the official campaigns for day-to-day material.

The *journalistic norm of 'objectivity'* (factor 8), understood as juxtaposing contrasting messages from the two official campaigns in order to maintain balance, was also dominant in television coverage of the EU referendum. According to Cushion and Lewis (2016), a third of the television news items they examined that involved statistics 'were tit-for-tat exchanges between rival camps, where journalists did not intervene one way or the other'. They found that broadcasters were even-handed in terms of giving both sides equal time, but did not scrutinise their claims. This might suggest that, like in the Scottish and the other referendums discussed in the previous chapter, broadcast journalists again adopted a *non-interventionist role* in the coverage (factor 1) and chose to juxtapose claims with opposing counter-claims from the official campaigns, thus 'sending' their frames within these messages.

BBC editorial guidelines for elections and referendums were revised in early 2016 and the new guidelines included a clause that explicitly discouraged journalists from interpreting due impartiality as equivalence between the two official campaigns and urged them to include perspectives from outside the official political camps:

Achieving due impartiality during the campaign means finding 'broad balance' between the arguments and not necessarily between the designated Campaign Groups. There may be circumstances in which other voices, beyond the formal representatives, are relevant to the arguments: these too should be weighed in terms of the broad balance. The designated Campaign Groups – whilst offering spokespeople to programme-makers and other content producers – cannot dictate who should or who should not appear on BBC output. (BBC Trust, 2016)

This means that this time there was more *distinction in broadcasting regulations* (at least as far as the BBC was concerned) between a referendum and an election campaign (factor 7), particularly relating to the inclusion of non-campaign sources in the coverage. Despite this, findings from research so far suggest that a seesaw approach to impartiality was implemented once again in English broadcasting (Cushion and Lewis, 2016). It is not possible to establish journalists' views of the value of the *game* frame in the 2016 referendum without further research, so factor 9 of the model is not possible to verify.

Apart from factors 7 and 9, therefore, all other factors in the frame-building model (Figure 3, page 141) seem to also have been at play in 2016. Journalists in print and broadcast media were heavily reliant on the two official campaigns, which both consisted of high-profile, powerful political actors who became the key regular figures of the campaigns, both sides promoted *policy* frames, and broadcasters particularly adopted a non-interventionist role in their coverage. All this, as the model suggests, may have contributed to the tendency of the mainstream media to reproduce official campaign frames in the 2016 referendum. In addition, the binary nature of the question, the fact that the referendum was conducted within established antagonistic (inner-)party politics, and the perception of objectivity as balance, which is deeply rooted in British broadcasting, may have additionally led to the use of the *game* frame, which as discussed earlier was also a very prominent interpretation of the referendum in the coverage.

Evidence appears to warrant the possibility that the same frame-building factors and the same framing of the campaign were repeated in UK-wide media in 2016, lending support to the model proposed in chapter 6. To prove causal relationships more research would be required, but the context of the coverage of the 2016 referendum appears to have been similar in the respects specified here to that described in the previous chapter of this book. That said, these similarities do not extend to the Scottish coverage of the 2016 EU referendum, which, as I will argue subsequently, was rather different from its English equivalent.

The framing of the 2016 EU referendum in Scotland

The main difference between the frame-building factors at play in the Scottish coverage of the 2016 EU referendum was the absence of significant elite framing or competition. Opinion polls had long shown that there was little support for leaving the EU among the electorate and as a result of this no major Scottish politicians backed the Leave campaign. The leaders of the SNP, Scottish Labour, Conservatives, Liberal Democrats and the Green Party all supported the Remain campaign while Leave had the support of much fewer and less prominent political actors from within and outside these parties. Discussion between politicians on Scottish channels was relatively rare and there appeared to be less effort invested in the media campaigns in Scotland.

Scottish broadcasting had considerably less coverage of the referendum produced specifically for Scottish audiences, compared to its UK-wide equivalent. As the BBC's daily evening bulletin *Reporting Scotland* was at 6.30 p.m., following after the UK-wide *News at Six*, the main referendum news each day was broadcast only in the London-produced bulletin. The Scottish bulletin featured only twenty-nine referendum items between 23 May and 23 June 2016, many of which explored the impact of a Leave or Remain vote on different policy areas that particularly affected Scotland (Dekavalla, forthcoming). Although there were occasionally clashes between politicians, this was not often the case. Much of the coverage examined the potential impact of a Leave or Remain outcome for Scotland, always maintaining balance between Leave and Remain perspectives. Of BBC *Reporting Scotland*'s coverage, 86.2 per cent thus contained the *policy* frame and just 31 per cent the *strategic game* frame (Dekavalla, forthcoming).

Although several of the Scottish bulletin items openly acknowledged the centrality of immigration and the economy in the 'referendum campaign', the bulletin engaged in frame-sending less than UK-wide media in 2016 and less than the Scottish media did during the 2014 Scottish referendum. Most of the items did carry the *policy* frame (as seen above) but many discussed policy areas such as farming, local manufacturing economy or fisheries, which (although still around the officially promoted *policy* frame) were outside the agenda of the mainstream campaigns. This could be because Scottish journalists were not as dependent on official campaigns for daily content this time and had less strong cues from Scottish politicians to guide them.

Although the issue was still binary and objectivity norms did apply (factors 5 and 8 in figure 3), the 2016 referendum was not conducted within established party politics in Scotland (factor 6) and there was not much material relating to elite competition to use in the stories (factor 9).

Although the EU referendum was binary, it was not contested in the Scottish public sphere. Public opinion polls led broadcasters to expect that there would be a pro-remain majority and that there was generally consensus among the public. As I argue elsewhere (Dekavalla, forthcoming), the EU referendum in Scotland fell within the outer borders of the sphere of legitimate controversy, and this allowed broadcasters to not focus on the competition of the campaign, since this latter was located on a different stage, in London.

As mentioned earlier in this chapter, BBC regulations this time did make more distinction between referendum and election coverage and this seems to have been taken into consideration in Scotland, where the BBC news bulletin gave space to a diversity of non-political perspectives. Based on these factors, it would thus appear to make sense that the *strategic game* frame was not particularly prominent in the Scottish bulletin. Clearly the data sample analysed here is limited due to the limited attention the referendum got on the specific Scottish news programme, and a larger sample would allow for a more reliable analysis, but the theorisation of frame-building in referendums proposed so far in this book appears to provide a plausible explanation for the construction of the 2016 referendum campaign on both Scottish and UK-wide media.

Framing campaigns in a multi-platform public sphere

This book has explored the media framing of referendum campaigns, with a particular focus on the way that mainstream journalists – and particularly broadcasters – select, construct and reproduce interpretations of what a referendum decision is about. It has proposed a new framework, in the form of an original model (Figure 3, page 141), to explain how news frames emerge during referendum campaigns and what factors may influence journalistic selection and adoption among the frames that are available in the public sphere. It has developed this framework based on findings from the present and previous studies of referendum campaigns in different contexts, and it has thus made an important contribution to literature on the mediation of the political process.

Frames as interpretative schemata, which help journalists tell stories and audiences understand what is at stake during a political event, are a particularly fruitful concept for analysing this process. This is because frames go beyond positive/negative tone assessment in news coverage, to explain how the media define issues in the public domain and how they propose the ways these issues should be thought about, which aspects of these issues are relevant in decision-making and which are not. The concept of framing as an interpretation of 'what is going on' allows

us to question taken-for-granted notions that may otherwise go unnoticed – for instance the notion that the political process is a game or that
national independence is about the future of the economy and the public
services. Thinking about these notions as frames draws our attention to
their constructed nature but also to the consequences such constructions
may have for decision-making and for citizens' understanding of their
own role in direct democracy initiatives.

This book has suggested that the media do not actively create original ways to understand referendum campaigns and there is little distinction between the way they report on elections and on referendums.
This means that they give the electorate a relatively restricted sense of
the power shift from political representatives to the public that direct
democracy involves. They clearly do emphasise the role of the public as
decision-makers (or voters) in direct democracy but not as shapers of
discourse and debate in the public sphere.

Digital media have long been hailed as carrying the potential to shift
discursive power from elites and politicians to ordinary people or to
groups whose voices are not normally heard in elite-dominated mainstream journalism. Indeed during the Scottish referendum digital media
played a very important role in the campaign and social media particularly served as platforms for grassroots politics to flourish and challenge
the 'old' media establishment (Law, 2015). However, as stressed in many
parts of this book, no political debate on any platform takes place in
a vacuum and there is significant interpenetration of discourses in different parts of the public sphere. Thus much of what was talked about
on mainstream 'old' media was also the topic of conversation on social
media, as seen in chapter 3.

Digital media however operate in different ways from mainstream
news organisations. The absence of journalists and media organisations as 'gatekeepers' on social media means that the representatives of
different political interests have direct access to digital platforms and
can use them to target voters, but also to falsify and mislead in order
to serve their purposes. Although, as argued in this book, traditional
media gatekeepers also allow substantial access to elite political parties
to frame issues in the news, the power of politicians in the mainstream
media is abated by pragmatic factors such as media regulation, ownership or journalistic professional routines. At least in Western countries, political elites do not have unrestricted power to determine public
discourse and their influence, although significant, is filtered by media
organisations.

On digital platforms, what news stories people are exposed to is determined by algorithms, not by traditional editorial decisions. Although

mainstream media organisations remain the most important source people use for news online and offline, there is a sense that journalists, their professional routines and values are becoming less central in the era of news aggregation, 'fake' news and social media. Traditional news organisations are now one of the voices available online – still a very powerful voice but one that is challenged by new ways of accessing and consuming news. This multiplicity of information may indeed make journalists' role even more vital in keeping to account not just political and economic authorities but also other sources of news. The interplay of dynamics between traditional news media and new online platforms is certainly a promising area of study.

Clearly though, what has been said in this book on frame-building only applies to traditional news media, with their formal structures, ownership patterns, business models, regulatory obligations, occupational role perceptions and special relationships with other establishment organisations in the political and economic spheres. These are the media that most framing research has focused on until now and they have so far occupied the centre of theoretical thinking around different media systems.

Yet developments in the last years suggest that political communication is changing and that mainstream media are no longer the only means for political sources to attempt to put across frames and messages. There is a sense that particularly events like the 2016 American election have undermined a lot of traditional thinking around the media. Future research on framing should thus also focus on digital communication processes and how messages are shaped outside the big institutional news gatekeepers. How are political events framed online? How do 'fake' news frames relate to mainstream news frames? How do Facebook algorithms relate to framing? How do social media produce news? In the future frame analysis will need to consider how it may account for the totality of news provision as this moves towards the internet and news aggregation, propaganda sites and social media.

This is not to undermine the significance of the processes studied in this book, which put frames onto the public arena through the 'old' media. These processes remain important because traditional news media are still key providers of news, whose content to a great extent determines public discourse across different platforms. Research on how framing works on new media however should complement these insights with an understanding of the shifting nature of public communication and information dissemination in contemporary Western democracies. This is especially significant in the current context of transformation and uncertainty, where much of what was taken for granted in politics, communication and democracy is put into question.

Finally, another point this book has attempted to demonstrate is that the news media are more than just direct mediators in the political process. Research in political studies very often represents political influence on media content and media influence on voters as rather direct and straightforward processes whereby politicians' messages eventually translate into public opinion shifts and the media are just the means through which this takes place. Often academic research on public opinion does not even mention the media as filters of elite messages – they are taken, by default, as direct channels of communication between politicians and voters. Framing theory problematises this assumption and draws our attention to the complexity involved in both journalists' adoption, adaptation or rejection of elite frames, as well as in audiences' adoption or rejection of media frames.

References

Aalberg, T., Strömbäck, J. and de Vreese, C. (2012) The framing of politics as strategy and game: A review of concepts, operationalizations and key findings. *Journalism*, 13(2): 162–178.

Altman, D. (2011) *Direct Democracy Worldwide*. New York: Cambridge University Press.

Anderson, B. (1983) *Imagined Communities: Reflections on the Origin and Spread of Nationalism*. London: Verso.

Atickan, E.O. (2015) *Framing the European Union: The Power of Political Arguments in Shaping European Integration*. Cambridge: Cambridge University Press.

Baden, C. and Lecheler, S. (2012) Fleeting, fading or far reaching? A knowledge-based model of the persistence of framing effects. *Communication Theory*, 22(4): 359–382.

Baker, K. and Norpoth, H. (1981) Candidates on television: The 1972 electoral debates in West Germany. *Public Opinion Quarterly*, 45: 329–345.

Balibar, E. (1991) The nation form. In Balibar, E. and Wallerstein, I. (eds) *Race, Nation, Class: Ambiguous Identities*. London: Verso, pp. 86–106.

Barford, V. (2014) Scotland votes 'No': How the 'No' side won the referendum. *BBC News*. Available at: www.bbc.co.uk/news/uk-29223984 (accessed 19 September 2014).

Bartholomé, G., Lecheler, S. and de Vreese, C. (2015) Manufacturing conflict? How journalists intervene in the conflict frame building process. *International Journal of Press/Politics*, 20(4): 438–457.

BBC Trust (2007) From seesaw to wagon wheel: Safeguarding impartiality in the 21st century. Available at: http://downloads.bbc.co.uk/bbctrust/assets/files/pdf/review_report_research/impartiality_21century/report.pdf (accessed 27 November 2016).

BBC Trust (2008) BBC network news coverage of the four UK nations. Available at: www.bbc.co.uk/bbctrust/our_work/editorial_standards/impartiality/network_news.html (accessed 6 January 2017).

BBC Trust (2016) BBC referendum guidelines 2016. Available at: www.bbc.co.uk/bbctrust/our_work/editorial_standards/eu_referendum (accessed 20 May 2017).

Bechhoffer, F. and McCrone, D. (2009) Stating the obvious: Ten truths about national identity. *Scottish Affairs*, 67: 7–22.

Bechtel, M., Hainmueller, J., Hangartner, D. and Helbing, M. (2015) Reality bites: The limits of framing effects in salient policy decisions. *Political Science Research and Methods*, 3(3): 559–582.

Bedingfield, S. and Anshari, D. (2014) Thinking about Romney: Frame building in a battleground state in the 2012 presidential election. *Journalism and Mass Communication Quarterly*, 91(1): 78–97.

Bennett, T. (1982) Theories of the media, theories of society. In Gurevitch, M., Bennett, T., Curran, J. and Woollacott, J. (eds) *Culture, Society and the Media*. New York: Methuen, pp. 26–51.

Bennett, W.L., Pickard, V., Iozzi, D., Schroeder, C., Lagos, T. and Caswell, C. (2004) Managing the public sphere: Journalistic construction of the great globalization debate. *Journal of Communication*, 54(3): 437–455.

Billig, M. (1995) *Banal Nationalism*. London: Sage.

Billig, M. (2009) Reflecting on a critical engagement with banal nationalism: Reply to Skey. *The Sociological Review*, 57(2): 347–352.

Billig, M., Downey, J., Richardson, J., Deacon, D. and Golding, P. (2005) 'Britishness' in the last three general elections: From ethnic to civic nationalism. Report for the Commission for Racial Equality.

Binder, M., Childers, M. and Johnson, N. (2015) Campaigns and the mitigation of framing effects of voting behavior: A natural and field experiment. *Political Behavior*, 37(3): 703–722.

Binderkrantz, A.S. and Green-Pedersen, C. (2009) Policy or processes in focus? *The International Journal of Press/Politics*, 14(2): 166–185.

Blain, N. and Hutchison, D. (2016) The media landscape in Scotland. In Blain, N. and Hutchison, D. (eds) *Scotland's Referendum and the Media: National and International Perspectives*. Edinburgh: Edinburgh University Press, pp. 16–25.

Blumler, J.G. and Gurevitch, M. (1995) *The Crisis of Public Communication*. London: Routledge.

Boesman, J., Berbers, A., d'Haenens, L. and Van Gorp, B. (2015) The news is in the frame: A journalist-centered approach to the frame-building process of the Belgian Syria fighters. *Journalism*, 18(3): 298–316.

Bond, R. (2006) Belonging and becoming: National identity and exclusion. *Sociology*, 40(4): 609–626.

Bond, R. and Rosie, M. (2002) National identities in post-devolution Scotland. *Scottish Affairs*, 40: 34–53.

Bond, R. and Rosie, M. (2006) Feeling Scottish: Its personal and political significance. Institute of Governance, Findings from the Leverhulme Trust's Research Programme on Nations and Regions, Identity Briefing no 3, January 2006. Available at: www.socsciscotland.ac.uk/__data/assets/pdf_file/0005/47354/IoG_Briefing_03.pdf (accessed 20 September 2017).

Bourdieu, P. (1991) *Language and Symbolic Power*. Cambridge: Polity Press.

Bransford, J.D. and Johnson, M.K. (1972) Contextual prerequisites for understanding. *Journal of Verbal Learning and Verbal Behaviour*, 11: 717–726.

Breuilly, J. (1985) *Nationalism and the State*. Chicago: University of Chicago Press.

Brewer, P. and Gross, K. (2010) Studying the effects of framing on public opinion about policy issues: Does what we see depend on how we look? In D'Angelo, P. and Kuypers, A. (eds) *Doing News Framing Analysis: Empirical and Theoretical Perspectives*. London: Routledge, pp. 159–186.

Brockliss, L. and Eastwood, D. (1997) Introduction. In Brockliss, L. and Eastwood, D. (eds) *A Union of Multiple Identities*. Manchester: Manchester University Press, pp. 1–8.

Brown, A., McCrone, D. and Paterson, L. (1998) *Politics and Society in Scotland*. London: Macmillan.

Brüggemann, M. (2014) Between frame setting and frame sending: How journalists contribute to news frames. *Communication Theory*, 24(1): 61–82.

Buchanan, M. (2016) 'Liked', 'shared', re-tweeted: The referendum campaign on social media. In Blain, N. and Hutchison, D. (eds) *Scotland's Referendum and the Media: National and International Perspectives*. Edinburgh: Edinburgh University Press, pp. 70–82.

Butler, D. and Ramney, A. (1994) Theory. In Butler, D. and Ramney, A. (eds) *Referendums Around the World: The Growing Use of Direct Democracy*. Basingstoke: Palgrave Macmillan, pp. 11–23.

Cacciatore, M., Scheufele, D. and Iyengar, S. (2016) The end of framing as we know it ... and the future of media effects. *Mass Communication and Society*, 19(1): 7–23.

Cappella, J. and Jamieson, K. (1997) *Spiral of Cynicism: The Press and the Public Good*. New York: Oxford University Press.

Castelló, E. and Capdevila, A. (2013) Defining pragmatic and symbolic frames: Newspapers about the independence during the Scottish and Catalan elections. *Estudios sobre el Mensaje Periodístico*, 19(2): 979–999.

Castelló, E. and Montagut, M. (2011) Journalists, reframing and party public relations consultants: Strategies in morning talk radio. *Journalism Studies*, 12(4): 506–521.

Chadwick, A. and Stanyer, J. (2011) The changing news media environment. In Heffernan, R., Cowley, P. and Hay, C. (eds) *Developments in British Politics*, Vol. 9. Basingstoke: Palgrave Macmillan, pp. 215–237.

Coleman, S. (1998) The televised leaders' debates in Britain: From talking heads to headless chickens. *Parliamentary Affairs*, 51(2): 182–197.

Colley, L. (1992) *Britons: Forging the Nation, 1707–1837*. New Haven: Yale University Press.

Connell, L. (2003) The Scottishness of the Scottish press: 1918–39. *Media, Culture and Society*, 25: 187–207.

Corbett, J. (2008) Scots, English and community languages in the Scottish media. In Blain, N. and Hutchison, D. (eds) *The Media in Scotland*. Edinburgh: Edinburgh University Press, pp. 20–34.

The Courier (2015, 19 October) BBC Scotland director rejects claims of 'unconscious bias' in independence referendum coverage. Available at: www.thecourier. co.uk/news/scotland/bbc-scotland-director-rejects-claims-of-unconscious-bias-in-independence-referendum-coverage-1.905922 (accessed 29 March 2016).

Craig, C. (1982) Myths against history: Tartanry and Kailyard in 19th-century Scottish literature. In McArthur, C. (ed.) *Scotch Reels: Scotland in Cinema and Television*. London: BFI Publishing, pp. 7–15.

Crespi, I. (1997) *The Public Opinion Process*. New Jersey: Lawrence Erlbaum Associates.

Cronin, T.E. (1989) *Direct Democracy: The Politics of Initiative, Referendum and Recall*. Cambridge, MA: Harvard University Press.

Curran, J. (1991) Rethinking the media as a public sphere. In Dahlgren, P. and Sparks, C. (eds) *Communication and Citizenship: Journalism and the Public Sphere*. New York: Routledge, pp. 27–57.

Curran, J. (2000) Rethinking media and democracy. In Curran, J. and Gurevitch, M. (eds) *Mass Media and Society*, third edition. London: Arnold, pp. 120–155.

Curran, J., Gurevitch, M., and Woollacott, J. (1982) The study of the media: Theoretical approaches. In Gurevitch, M., Bennett, T., Curran, J. and Woollacott, J. (eds) *Culture, Society and the Media*. New York: Methuen, pp. 6–25.

Curtice, J. (2005) Brought together or driven apart? In Miller, W. (ed.) *Anglo-Scottish Relations from 1900 to Devolution and Beyond*. Oxford: Oxford University Press, pp. 151–170.

Curtice, J. (2014, 18 February) So where does Scotland stand on more devolution? Scotcen report available at: www.scotcen.org.uk/blog/what-does-scotland-think-about-more-devolution (accessed 6 November 2014).

Cushion, S. and Lewis, J. (2016) Scrutinising statistical claims and constructing balance: Television news coverage of the 2016 EU referendum. In Jackson, D., Thorsen, E. and Wring, D. (eds) *EU Referendum Analysis 2016: Media, Voters and the Campaign*. Poole: CSJCC Bournemouth University, p. 40.

Cushion, S. and Thomas, R. (2017) From quantitative precision to qualitative judgements: Professional perspectives about the impartiality of television news during the 2015 UK General Election. *Journalism* (online first) DOI: 10.1177/1464884916685909.

Cushion, S., Thomas, R., Kilby, A., Morani, M. and Sambrook, R. (2016) Interpreting the media logic behind editorial decisions: Television news coverage of the 2015 UK general election campaign. *International Journal of Press/Politics*, 21(4): 472–489.

D'Angelo, P. (2002) News framing as a multiparadigmatic research programme: A response to Entman. *Journal of Communication*, 52(4): 870–888.

Dahlgren, P. (1991) Introduction. In Dahlgren, P. and Sparks, C. (eds) *Communication and Citizenship: Journalism and the Public Sphere*. London: Routledge, pp. 1–23.

Dahlgren, P. (2006) Civic participation and practices: Beyond 'deliberative democracy'. In *Researching Media, Democracy and Participation: The Intellectual Work of the 2006 European Media and Communication Doctoral Summer School*. Estonia: Tartu University Press, pp. 23–34.

Dalton, R.J. (2002) *Citizen Politics: Public Opinion and Political Parties in Advanced Industrial Democracies*. New York: Chatham House.

de Cillia, R., Reisigl, M. and Wodak, R. (1999) The discursive construction of national identities. *Discourse and Society*, 10: 149–173.

de Vreese, C. (2004) The effects of frames in political television news on issue interpretation and frame salience. *Journalism and Mass Communication Quarterly*, 81(1): 36–52.

de Vreese, C. (2012) New avenues for framing research. *American Behavioral Scientist*, 56(3): 365–375.

de Vreese, C. and Semetko, H. (2002) Cynical and engaged: Strategic campaign coverage, public opinion, and mobilization in a referendum. *Communication Research*, 29(6): 615–641.

de Vreese, C. and Semetko, H. (2004) *Political Campaigning in Referendums: Framing the Referendum Issue*. Abingdon: Routledge.

de Vreese, C., Peter, J. and Semetko, H. (2001) Framing politics at the launch of the Euro: A cross-national comparative study of frames in the news. *Political Communication*, 18: 107–122.

Deacon, D., Downey, J., Harmer, E., Stanyer, J. and Wring, D. (2016) The narrow agenda: How the news media covered the referendum. In Jackson, D., Thorsen, E. and Wring, D. (eds) *EU Referendum Analysis 2016: Media, Voters and the Campaign*. Poole: CSJCC Bournemouth University, p. 34.

Dekavalla, M. (2012) Evaluating newspaper performance in the public sphere: Press accounts of Westminster elections in Scotland and in England in the early post-devolution period. *Journalism*, 13(3): 320–339.

Dekavalla, M. (2015) The Scottish newspaper industry in the digital era. *Media, Culture and Society*, 37(1): 107–114.

Dekavalla, M. (2016) The Scottish press account: Discourses of independence. In Blain, N., Hutchison, D. and Hassan, G. (eds) *Scotland's Referendum and the Media: National and International Perspectives*. Edinburgh: Edinburgh University Press, pp. 46–58.

Dekavalla, M. (forthcoming) The EU referendum on Scottish television. In Leon-Solis, F., O'Donnell, H. and Ridge-Newman, A. (eds) *Britain's EU Referendum and the Media: National and International Perspectives*. London: Palgrave.

Dekavalla, M. and Jelen-Sanchez, A. (2016) Whose voices are heard in the news? A study of sources in television coverage of the Scottish independence referendum. *British Politics*. Epub ahead of print 20 September. DOI: 10.1057/s41293-016-0026-4.

Denver, D. (2002) Voting in the 1997 Scottish and Welsh devolution referendums: Information, interests and opinions. *European Journal of Political Research*, 41: 827–843.

Deutsch, K.W. (1953) *Nationalism and Social Communication*. Cambridge, MA: MIT.

Devine, T.M. (1999) *The Scottish Nation: 1700–2000*. London: Penguin.

Devine, T.M. (2016) *Independence or Union: Scotland's Past and Scotland's Present*. Edinburgh: Edinburgh University Press.

Dimitrova, D. and Strömbäck, J. (2011) Election news in Sweden and the United States: A comparative study of sources and media frames. *Journalism*, 13(5): 604–619.

Druckman, J.N. (2001) The implications of framing effects for citizen competence. *Political Behaviour*, 23(3): 225–256.

Druckman, J.N. (2004) Political preference formation: Competition, deliberation, and the (ir)relevance of framing effects. *American Political Science Review*, 98(4): 671–686.

Dunaway, J. (2008) Markets, ownership, and the quality of campaign news coverage. *Journal of Politics*, 70(4): 1193–1202.

Dunaway, J. and Lawrence, R. (2015) What predicts the game frame? Media ownership, electoral context, and campaign news. *Political Communication*, 32(1): 43–60.

Electoral Commission (2014) Scottish Independence Referendum: Report on the referendum held on 18 September 2014. Available at: www.electoralcommission.org.uk/__data/assets/pdf_file/0010/179812/Scottish-independence-referendum-report.pdf (accessed 4 September 2016).

Elster, J. (1998) Introduction. In Elster, J. (ed.) *Deliberative Democracy*. New York: Cambridge University Press, pp. 1–18.

Entman, R. (1993) Framing: Toward clarification of a fractured paradigm. *Journal of Communication*, 43(4): 51–58.

Evans, G. and Trystan, D. (1999) Why was 1997 different? A comparative analysis of the 1979 and 1997 Welsh referendums. In Taylor, B. and Thomson, K. (eds) Scotland and Wales: Nations Again? Cardiff: University of Wales Press, pp. 95–117.

Fang, A., Ounis, I., Habel, P., Macdonald, C. and Limsopatham, N. (2015) Topic-centric classification of Twitter users' political orientation. Proceedings of the 38th Annual International ACM SIGIR Conference on Research and Development in Information Retrieval. Available at: http://terrierteam.dcs.gla.ac.uk/publications/fang2015sigir.pdf (accessed 6 January 2017).

Feree, M.M., Gamson, W.A., Gerhards, J. and Rucht, D. (2002) *Shaping Abortion Discourse: Democracy and the Public Sphere in Germany and the United States*. New York: Cambridge University Press.

Gamson, W.A. (2001) Promoting political engagement. In Bennett, W.L. and Entman, R.M. (eds) *Mediated Politics: Communication and the Future of Democracy*. New York: Cambridge University Press, pp. 56–74.

Gamson, W.A. and Modigliani, A. (1987) The changing culture of affirmative action. In Braungart, R.G. and Braungart, M.M. (eds) *Research in Political Sociology*, Vol. 3. Greenwich, CT: Jai Press, pp. 137–177.

Gamson, W.A. and Modigliani, A. (1989) Media discourse and public opinion on nuclear power: A constructionist approach. *American Journal of Sociology*, 95: 1–37.

Garton, G., Montgomery, M. and Tolson, A. (1991) Ideology, scripts and metaphors in the public sphere of a general election. In Scannell, P. (ed.) *Broadcast Talk*. London: Sage, pp. 100–118.

Gellner, E. (1983) *Nations and Nationalism*. Oxford: Basil Blackwell.

Gerth, M. and Siegert, G. (2012) Patterns of consistence and constriction: How news media frame the coverage of direct democratic campaigns. *American Behavioral Scientist*, 56(3): 279–299.

Goffman, E. (1974). *Frame Analysis: An Essay on the Organisation of Experience*. New York: Harper Colophon.

Guibernau, M. and Goldblatt, D. (2000) Identity and nation. In Woodward, K. (ed.) *Questioning Identity: Gender, Class, Nation*. London: Routledge, pp. 115–154.

Habermas, J. (1989) *The Structural Transformation of the Public Sphere*. Cambridge: Polity Press.

Hackett, R.A. (2005) Is there a democratic deficit in US and UK journalism? In Allan, S. (ed.) *Journalism: Critical Issues*. Maidenhead: McGraw-Hill, pp. 85–97.

Hall, S. (1982) The rediscovery of 'ideology': Return of the repressed in media studies. In Gurevitch, M., Bennett, T., Curran, J. and Woollacott, J. (eds) *Culture, Society and the Media*. New York: Methuen, pp. 52–86.

Hall, S. (1992) The question of cultural identity. In Hall, S., Held, D. and McGrew, T. (eds) *Modernity and its Futures*. Cambridge: Polity Press, pp. 274–316.

Hall, S., Critcher, T., Jefferson, T., Clarke, J. and Roberts, B. (1978) *Policing the Crisis: Mugging, the State and Law and Order*. Basingstoke: Macmillan Press.

Hallin, D. and Mancini, P. (2004) *Comparing Media Systems: Three Models of Media and Politics*. Cambridge: Cambridge University Press.

Hanggli, R. (2012) Key factors in frame building: How strategic political actors shape news media coverage. *American Behavioral Scientist*, 56(3): 300–317.

Hanggli, R. and Kriesi, H. (2010) Political framing strategies and their impact on media framing in a Swiss direct-democratic campaign. *Political Communication*, 27(2): 141–157.

Hanggli, R. and Kriesi, H. (2012) Frame construction and frame promotion (strategic framing choices). *American Behavioral Scientist*, 56(3): 260–278.

Hanitzsch, T. (2007) Deconstructing journalism culture: Towards a universal theory. *Communication Theory*, 17: 367–385.

Hanitzsch, T. and Mellado, C. (2011) What shapes the news around the world? How journalists in eighteen countries perceive influences on their work. *International Journal of Press/Politics*, 16(3): 404–426.

Hanitzsch, T. and Vos, T. (2016) Journalism beyond democracy: A new look into journalistic roles in political and everyday life. *Journalism*, online first. DOI: 10.1177/1464884916673386.

Hanitzsch, T., Hanusch, F., Mellado, C., *et al.* (2011) Mapping journalism cultures across nations: A comparative study of 18 countries. *Journalism Studies*, 12(3): 273–293.

Harcup, T., and O'Neil, D. (2001) What is news? Galtung and Ruge revisited. *Journalism Studies*, 2(2): 261–280.

Hassan, G. (2014) *Independence of the Scottish Mind.* Basingstoke: Palgrave Macmillan.

Hearn, J. (2012) *Theorizing Power.* Basingstoke: Palgrave Macmillan.

Heath, A. and Taylor, B. (1999) Were the Scottish and Welsh referendums second-order elections? In Taylor, B. and Thomson, K. (eds) *Scotland and Wales: Nations Again?* Cardiff: University of Wales Press, pp. 149–168.

Heilman, R. and Miclea, M. (2016) Risk seeking preferences: An investigation of framing effects across decisional domains. *Cognition, Brain, Behavior*, 20(1): 1–17.

Hopmann, D., Van Aelst, P. and Legnante, G. (2011) Political balance in the news: A review of concepts, operationalizations and key findings. *Journalism*, 13(2): 240–257.

Hutchison, D. (2008) The history of the press. In Blain, N. and Hutchison, D. (eds) *The Media in Scotland.* Edinburgh: Edinburgh University Press, pp. 55–70.

Independent (2014, 16 September) Scottish independence: Full text of David Cameron's 'no going back' speech. Available at: www.independent.co.uk/news/uk/scottish-independence/scottish-independence-full-text-of-david-camerons-no-going-back-speech-9735902.html (accessed 30 September 2016).

Irwin, G. and Van Holsteyn, J. (2008) What are they waiting for? Strategic information for late deciding voters. *International Journal of Public Opinion Research*, 20(4): 483–493.

Iyengar, S., Norpoth, H. and Kahn, S. (2004) Consumer demand for election news: The horserace sells. *The Journal of Politics*, 66(1): 157–175.

Jamieson, K.H. (1992) *Dirty Politics.* New York: Oxford University Press.

Jenkins, R. (1996) *Social Identity.* London: Routledge.

Johns, R. and Mitchell, J. (2016) *Takeover: Explaining the Extraordinary Rise of the SNP.* London: Biteback.

Jones, P. (1992) Politics. In Linklater, M. and Denniston, R. (eds) *Anatomy of Scotland: How Scotland Works.* Edinburgh: W&R Chambers.

Jones, P. (1997) A start to a new song: The 1997 devolution referendum campaign. *Scottish Affairs*, 21: 1–16.

Jones, P. (2008) Scotland: The nationalist phoenix. In Trench, A. (ed.) *The State of the Nations 2008.* Exeter: Imprint, pp. 23–55.

Keaveney, P. (2016) Notes for editors: What press releases tell us about Vote Leave and Britain Stronger in Europe. In Jackson, D., Thorsen, E. and Wring, D. (eds) *EU Referendum Analysis 2016: Media, Voters and the Campaign.* Poole: CSJCC Bournemouth University, p. 75.

Keith, S. (2011) Shifting circles: Reconceptualizing Shoemaker and Reese's theory of a hierarchy of influences on media content for a newer media era. *Web Journal of Mass Communication Research*, 29: 1.

Kidd, C. (1997) Sentiment, race and revival: Scottish identities in the aftermath of enlightenment. In Brockliss, L. and Eastwood, D. (eds) *A Union of Multiple Identities*. Manchester: Manchester University Press, pp. 110–126.

Kiely, R., Bechhoffer, F. and McCrone, D. (2005) Birth, blood and belonging: Identity claims in post-devolution Scotland. *The Sociological Review*: 150–171.

Kinder, D. (2007) Curmudgeonly advice. *Journal of Communication*, 57: 155–162.

Kothari, A. (2010) The framing of the Darfur conflict in the *New York Times*: 2003–2006. *Journalism Studies*, 11(2): 209–224.

Kumar, K. (2003) *The Making of English National Identity*. Cambridge: Cambridge University Press.

Kvale, S. (1996) *InterViews: An Introduction to Qualitative Research Interviewing*. Thousand Oaks: Sage.

Law, A. (2015) Mediating the Scottish independence debate. *Media Education Journal*, 56: 3–7.

Lawrence, R. (2000) Game-framing the issues: Tracking the strategy frame in public policy news. *Political Communication*, 17(2): 93–114.

Lawrence, R. (2010) Researching political news framing. In D'Angelo, P. and Kuypers, A. (eds) *Doing News Framing Analysis: Empirical and Theoretical Perspectives*. New York: Routledge, pp. 265–287.

Lecheler, S. and de Vreese, C.H. (2011) Getting real: The duration of framing effects. *Journal of Communication*, 61: 959–983.

LeDuc, L. (2002) Referendums and elections: How do campaigns differ? In Farrell, D. and Schmitt-Beck, R. (eds) *Do Political Campaigns Matter? Campaign Effects in Elections and Referendums*. London: Routledge, pp. 145–162.

LeDuc, L. (2015) Referendums and deliberative democracy. *Electoral Studies*, 38: 139–148.

Lewis, J., Inthorn, J. and Wahl-Jorgensen, K. (2005) *Citizens or Consumers? What the Media Tell Us About Political Participation*. Maidenhead: Open University Press.

Lippmann, W. (1922) *Public Opinion*. London: Macmillan.

McArthur, C. (1981) Breaking the signs: Scotch myths as cultural struggle. *Cencrastus*, 7: 21–25.

McCrone, D. (2000) Scotland and the union: Changing identities in the British state. In Morley, D. and Robins, K. (eds) *British Cultural Studies*. Oxford: Oxford University Press, pp. 97–108.

McCrone, D. (2001) *Understanding Scotland: The Sociology of a Nation*, second edition. London: Routledge.

McCrone, D. (2005a) W(h)ither the union? In Miller, W. (ed.) *Anglo-Scottish Relations from 1900 to Devolution and Beyond*. Oxford: Oxford University Press, pp. 203–220.

McCrone, D. (2005b) Cultural capital in an understated nation: The case of Scotland. *The British Journal of Sociology*, 56(1): 65–82.

McCrone, D. and Lewis, B. (1999) The Scottish and Welsh referendum campaigns. In Taylor, B. and Thomson, K. (eds) *Scotland and Wales: Nations Again?* Cardiff: University of Wales Press, pp. 17–40.

McNair, B. (2008) The Scottish media and politics. In Blain, N. and Hutchison, D. (eds) *The Media in Scotland.* Edinburgh: Edinburgh University Press, pp. 227–242.

McNair, B., Dekavalla, M., Boyle, R. and Meikle, G. (2010) Mapping futures for news: Trends, opportunities and challenges for Scotland. Report for the Scottish Universities Insight Institute.

Mendelsohn, M. (1993) Television's frames in the 1988 Canadian election. *Canadian Journal of Communication,* 18(2): 149–171.

Mitchell, J. (2016a) The referendum campaign. In McHarg, A., Mullen, T., Page, A. and Walker, N. (eds) *The Scottish Independence Referendum: Constitutional and Political Implications.* Oxford: Oxford University Press, pp. 75–95.

Mitchell, J. (2016b) The unexpected campaign. In Blain, N. and Hutchison, D. (eds) *Scotland's Referendum and the Media: National and International Perspectives.* Edinburgh: Edinburgh University Press, pp. 3–15.

Mullen, T. (2016) Introduction. In McHarg, A., Mullen, T., Page, A. and Walker, N. (eds) *The Scottish Independence Referendum: Constitutional and Political Implications.* Oxford: Oxford University Press, pp. 3–27.

Murkens, J. (2002) Preliminary issues. In Murkens, J., Jones, P. and Keating, M. (eds) *Scottish Independence: A Practical Guide.* Edinburgh: Edinburgh University Press, pp. 9–42.

Nairn, T. (1977) *The Break-Up of Britain.* London: Verso.

Nisbet, M. (2010) Knowledge into action: Framing the debates over climate change and poverty. In D'Angelo, P. and Kuypers, J. (eds) *Doing News Framing Analysis: Empirical and Theoretical Perspectives.* New York: Routledge, pp. 43–83.

Norris, P. and Sanders, D. (1998) Does balance matter? Experiments in TV news. Paper presented at at the Annual Meeting of the American Political Science Association, Boston, 3–6 September 1998.

Ofcom (2013) Broadcasting code guidance notes – Section 6: Elections and referendums. Available at: http://stakeholders.ofcom.org.uk/binaries/broadcast/guidance/831193/section6. pdf (accessed 3 January 2016).

Ofcom (2015) Adults' media use and attitudes. Report May 2015. Available at: http://stakeholders.ofcom.org.uk/market-data-research/other/research-publications/adults/media-lit-10years/ (accessed 25 February 2016).

Pammett, J.H. and LeDuc, L. (2001) Sovereignty, leadership and voting in the Quebec referendums. *Electoral Studies,* 20: 265–280.

Paterson, L. (1981) Scotch myths. *Bulletin of Scottish Politics,* 1(2): 67–71.

Paterson, L. (2015) Utopian pragmatism: Scotland's choice. *Scottish Affairs,* 24(1): 22–46.

Paterson, L. and Wyn Jones, R. (1999) Does civil society drive constitutional change? In Taylor, B. and Thomson, K. (eds) *Scotland and Wales: Nations Again?* Cardiff: University of Wales Press, pp. 169–197.

Paterson, L., Brown, A., Curtice, J., Hinds, K., McCrone, D., Park, A., Sprotson, K. and Surridge, P. (2001) *New Scotland, New Politics?* Edinburgh: Polygon.

Patterson, T.E. (1980) *The Mass Media Election: How Americans Choose Their President.* New York: Praeger.

Patterson, T.E. (1993) *Out of Order.* New York: Knopf.

Patterson, T.E. (1998) Political roles of the journalist. In Graber, D., McQuail, D. and Norris, P. (eds) *The Politics of News – the News of Politics.* Washington, DC: CQ Press, pp. 17–32.

Pedersen, R. (2014) News media framing of negative campaigning. *Mass Communication and Society*, 17(6): 898–919.

Peters, B. (2008) National and transnational public spheres. In Wessler, H. (ed.) *Public Deliberation and Public Culture: The Writings of Bernard Peters 1993–2005.* Basingstoke: Palgrave Macmillan, pp. 185–196.

Pittock, M.G.H. (1999) *Celtic Identity and the British Image.* Manchester: Manchester University Press.

Plunkett, J. (2014, 26 August) Scottish independence TV debate watched by more than 2 million. *Guardian*. Available at: www.theguardian.com/media/2014/aug/26/scottish-independence-tv-debate-bbc2-salmond-darling (accessed 20 September 2017).

Price, V., Tewksbury, D. and Powers, E. (1997) Switching trains of thought: The impact of news frames on readers' cognitive responses. *Communication Research*, 24(5): 481–506.

Quinlan, S., Shephard, M. and Paterson, L. (2015) Online discussion and the 2014 Scottish independence referendum: Flaming keyboards or forums for deliberation? *Electoral Studies*, 38: 192–205.

Qvortrup, M. (2014) Introduction: Theory, practice and history. In Qvortrup, M. (ed.) *Referendums Around the World: The Continued Growth of Direct Democracy.* Basingstoke: Palgrave Macmillan, pp. 1–17.

Reese, S. (2007) Journalism research and the hierarchy of influences model: A global perspective. *Brazilian Journalism Research*, 3(2): 29–42.

Reuters Institute for the Study of Journalism (2015) Sources of news. Digital News Report 2015. Available at: www.digitalnewsreport.org/survey/2015/sources-of-news-2015/ (accessed 4 March 2016).

Riley-Smith, B. (2014, 14 September) Scottish independence: Nationalists demand Nick Robinson sacking in vocal anti-BBC protest. *Telegraph*. Available at: www.telegraph.co.uk/news/uknews/Scottish-independence/11095752/Scottish-independence-Nationalists-demand-Nick-Robinson-sacking-in-vocal-anti-BBC-protest.html (accessed 20 September 2017).

Robinson, G. (1998) *Constructing the Quebec Referendum: French and English Media Voices.* Toronto: University of Toronto Press.

Schemer, C., Wirth, W. and Matthes, J. (2012) Value resonance and value framing effects on voting intentions in direct-democratic campaigns. *American Behavioral Scientist*, 56(3): 334–352.

Scheufele, D. (1999) Framing as a theory of media effects. *Journal of Communication*, 49(1): 103–122.

Schlesinger, P. (1990) Rethinking the sociology of journalism: Source strategies and the limits of media centrism. In Ferguson, M. (ed.) *Public Communication: The New Imperatives*. London: Sage, pp. 61–83.

Schlesinger, P. (1998) Scottish devolution and the media. In Seaton, J. (ed.) *Politics and the Media: Harlots and Prerogatives at the Turn of the Millennium*. Oxford: Blackwell, pp. 55–74.

Schlesinger, P. (2000) The nation and communicative space. In Tumber, H. (ed.) *Media, Power, Professionals and Policies*. London: Routledge, pp. 99–115.

Schlesinger, P., Miller, D. and Dinan, W. (2001) *Open Scotland? Journalists, Spin Doctors and Lobbyists*. Edinburgh: Polygon.

Schudson, M. (1995) *The Power of News*. Cambridge, MA: Harvard University Press.

Schudson, M. (2001) The objectivity norm in American journalism. *Journalism*, 2(2): 149–170.

Semetko, H.A. and Valkenburg, P.M. (2000) Framing European politics: A content analysis of press and television news. *Journal of Communication*, 50(2): 93–109.

Shah, D.V., Domke, D. and Wackman, D.B. (1996) To thine own self be true: Values, framing, and voter decision-making strategies. *Communication Research*, 23(5): 509–560.

Shephard, M. (2014, 16 September) Is the 'Yes' online tsunami finally paying dividends? Available at: http://blog.whatscotlandthinks.org/2014/09/yes-online-tsunami-finally-paying-dividends/ (accessed 20 September 2017).

Shephard, M. and Johns, R. (2012) A face for radio? How viewers and listeners reacted differently to the third leaders' debate in 2010. *The British Journal of Politics and International Relations*, 14: 1–18.

Shoemaker, P.J. and Reese, S.D. (2014) *Mediating the Message in the 21st Century: A Media Sociology Perspective*, third edition. New York: Routledge.

Simmel, G. (1997) The sociology of space. In Frisby, D. and Featherstone, M. (eds) *Simmel on Culture: Selected Writings*. London: Sage, pp. 137–170.

Simon, A. and Xenos, M. (2000) Media framing and effective public deliberation. *Political Communication*, 17: 363–376.

Skovsgaard, M., Albaek, E., Bro, P. and de Vreese, C. (2013) A reality check: How journalists' role perceptions impact their implementation of the objectivity norm. *Journalism*, 14(1): 22–42.

Slothuus, R. (2008) More than weighting cognitive importance: A dual process model of issue framing effects. *Political Psychology*, 29(1): 1–28.

Snow, D.A. and Benford, R.D. (1988) Ideology, frame resonance and participant mobilization. In Klandermans, B., Kriesi, H. and Tarrow, S. (eds) *From Structure to Action: Social Movement Participation Across Cultures*. Greenwich, CT: JAI Press, pp. 197–218.

Sparks, C. (1991) Goodbye, Hildy Johnson: The vanishing serious press. In Dahlgren, P. and Sparks, C. (eds) *Communication and Citizenship: Journalism and the Public Sphere*. London: Routledge, pp. 58–74.

Strömbäck, J. (2005) In search of a standard: Four models of democracy and their normative implications for journalism. *Journalism Studies*, 6(3): 331–345.

Strömbäck, J. and Dimitrova, D. (2006) Political and media systems matter: A comparison of election news coverage in Sweden and the United States. *International Journal of Press/Politics*, 11(4): 131–147.

Strömbäck, J. and Kaid, L.L. (eds) (2008) *Handbook of Election News Coverage around the World*. New York: Routledge.

Strömbäck, J. and Van Aelst, P. (2010) Exploring some antecedents of the media's framing of election news: A comparison of Swedish and Belgian election news. *International Journal of Press/Politics*, 15(1): 41–59.

Tandoc, E. (2015) Reframing gatekeeping: How passing gates reshapes news frames. *Asia Pacific Media Educator*, 25(1): 121–136.

Taylor, P.J. (2000) Which Britain? Which England? Which North? In Morley, D. and Robins, K. (eds) *British Cultural Studies*. Oxford: Oxford University Press, pp. 127–144.

Tewksbury, D., Jones, J., Peske, M., Raymond, A. and Vig, W. (2000) The interaction of news and advocate frames: Manipulating audience perceptions of a local public policy issue. *Journalism and Mass Communication Quarterly*, 77(4): 804–829.

Tierney, S. (2012) *Constitutional Referendums: The Theory and Practice of Republican Deliberation*. Oxford: Oxford University Press.

TNS-BMRB (2014) Which issue is most important to you in deciding how to vote in the referendum? Survey findings available at: http://whatscotland-thinks.org/questions/which-issue-is-most-important-to-you-in-deciding-how-to-vote-in-the-referendum (accessed 20 September 2017).

Trench, A. (2008) Introduction: The second phase of devolution. In Trench, A. (ed.) *The State of the Nations 2008*. Exeter: Imprint, pp. 1–22.

Tuchman, G. (1972) Objectivity as strategic ritual: An examination of newsmen's notions of objectivity. *American Journal of Sociology*, 77(4): 660–679.

van Dalen, A., de Vreese, C. and Albaek, E. (2012) Different roles, different content? A four-country comparison of the role conceptions and reporting style of political journalists. *Journalism*, 13(7): 903–922.

van Dijk, T. (1995) Power and the news media. In Paletz, D. (ed.) *Political Communication and Action*. Cresskill: Hampton Press, pp. 9–36.

Verstraeten, H. (1996) The media and the transformation of the public sphere: A contribution for a critical political economy of the public sphere. *European Journal of Communication*, 11(3): 347–370.

Vos, T. (2011) A mirror of the times: A history of the mirror metaphor in journalism. *Journalism Studies*, 12(5): 575–589.

Wahl-Jorgensen, K., Berry, M., Garcia-Blanco, I., Bennett, L. and Cable, J. (2016) Rethinking balance and impartiality in journalism? How the BBC attempted and failed to change the paradigm. *Journalism*, 18(7): 781–800.

Wahl-Jorgensen, K., Sambrook, R., Berry, M., Moore, K., Bennett, L., Cable, J., Garcia-Blanco, I., Kidd, J., Dencik, L. and Hintz, A. (2013) BBC breadth of

opinion review content analysis. Report available at: http://downloads.bbc.
co.uk/bbctrust/assets/files/pdf/our_work/breadth_opinion/content_analysis.
pdf (accessed 27 November 2016).

Wallerstein, I. (1991) The construction of peoplehood: Racism, nationalism, ethnicity. In Balibar, E. and Wallerstein, I. (eds) *Race, Nation, Class: Ambiguous
Identities*. London: Verso, pp. 71–85.

Wettstein, M. (2012) Frame adoption in referendum campaigns: The effect
of news coverage on the public salience of issue interpretations. *American
Behavioural Scientist*, 56(3): 318–333.

Williams, K. (2003) *Understanding Media Theory*. London: Bloomsbury
Academic.

Winetrobe, B. and Hazell, R. (2005) What has the Scottish Parliament achieved
and what can it teach Westminster? In Miller, W. (ed.) *Anglo-Scottish
Relations from 1900 to Devolution and Beyond*. Oxford: Oxford University
Press, pp. 63–77.

YouGov (2014, 6 September) 'Yes' campaign lead at 2 in Scottish Referendum.
Available at: https://yougov.co.uk/news/2014/09/06/latest-scottish-referendum-
poll-yes-lead (accessed 22 October 2016).

Zelizer, B. (2005) Definitions of journalism. In Overholser, G. and Jamieson,
K. (eds) *Institutions of American Democracy: The Press*. New York: Oxford
University Press, pp. 66–80.

Index

EU authorised representative for GPSR:
Easy Access System Europe, Mustamäe tee 50,
10621 Tallinn, Estonia
gpsr.requests@easproject.com

www.ingramcontent.com/pod-product-compliance
Lightning Source LLC
Chambersburg PA
CBHW050515280326
41932CB00014B/2328